ARE YOU IN DANGER OF THE WENDY TRAP?

How Often Do You Ask Yourself . . .

Why do I feel like his mother?
Why do things always go his way?
Why can't I depend upon him?
Why can't he love me the way I love him?
What did I do to deserve this?
Why can't I make him change?
What would he do if he didn't have me to take care of him?
Couldn't I have spotted these problems sooner?
What if he won't change?

Dr. Kiley's *Wendy Test* in Chapter 2 helps you look at your own feelings and behavior to see if inappropriate mothering dominates your relationship, and puts you in danger of falling into the *Wendy Trap*.

Other Avon Books by
Dr. Dan Kiley

THE PETER PAN SYNDROME: MEN WHO
NEVER GROW UP

DR. DAN'S PRESCRIPTIONS: 1001 NONMEDICAL HINTS
FOR SOLVING PARENTING PROBLEMS

THE WENDY DILEMMA

WHEN WOMEN STOP MOTHERING THEIR MEN

Dr. Dan Kiley

AVON
PUBLISHERS OF BARD, CAMELOT, DISCUS AND FLARE BOOKS

AVON BOOKS
A division of
The Hearst Corporation
1790 Broadway
New York, New York 10019

The Arbor House edition contains the following Library of Congress
Cataloging in Publication data:

Kiley, Dan.
  The Wendy dilemma.

  Bibliography: p.
  1. Wives—United States—Psychology. 2. Men—United
States—Psychology. 3. Marriage—United States
4. Interpersonal relations. I. Title.
HQ759.K53 1984   155.6′32   84-12325

First Avon Printing, September 1985

To the many women
who've helped me understand

Contents

RESOLVING THE WENDY DILEMMA 143

Introduction

Talking with thousands of women across the country as well as in private counseling sessions, I've noticed the same conversation repeating itself.

"I just don't know what to do with him anymore."

"How's that?"

"My man—he just can't take care of himself."

"What do you mean?"

"If I didn't make sure he had something to eat, he'd starve. And if I didn't give in to him, his temper tantrums might cause him to have a heart attack."

"You're acting just like his mother."

"Don't I know it!"

During the course of our conversation, most of these women admit that they detest playing the role of mother to men. They want it to stop. But they feel trapped. On the one hand, they realize that mothering a man encourages immature behavior; on the other, mothering him sometimes seems like the best way to express love. They want to stop mothering without abandoning their love. When a woman wants to care and protect her man without falling into the trap of mothering him, she faces a dilemma, *The Wendy Dilemma*. Wendy, as you recall, was a character in J. M. Barrie's play who was constantly mothering the childlike Peter Pan.

Women trapped in this dilemma, or in danger of being trapped, face several internal battles: the traditional feminine role versus personal freedom, self-promotion versus self-sacrifice, and short-term versus long-term goals.

Resolution of the dilemma is possible with thoughtful self-examination and the courage to grow into a new kind of person.

Some women are immobilized by the Wendy Dilemma. They suffer from a distorted notion of control. Because of an immaturity that prevents them from gaining mastery over their own lives, they adopt attitudes and behaviors that make them feel they are controlling the lives of others. Nowhere is this pattern more evident than in their intimate relationship with a man. Mothering becomes the key strategy in their attempt to gain some semblance of adult control.

That the mother role-playing is the woman's way of avoiding growing up and taking responsibility for adult relationships is the sad irony of the Wendy Dilemma. Having placed all of the blame for a troubled relationship on the man, she need not subject herself to painful examination of her own unhealthy communication and behavior patterns.

Soon, however, the man refuses to accept the blame, and the woman is forced to take it all—and then some—back onto herself. This is when she begins to be plagued by self-doubt. Her efforts to solve her problems meet with little or no success, and she ends up worse off for her efforts. To her, and women like her, a resolution of the Wendy Dilemma seems impossible, and they develop strategies not to escape the trap, but simply to survive.

Women trapped in the Wendy Dilemma keep one figurative foot in the playpen as they venture into the adult world. The result is a dual behavior pattern in which they pretend to be worldly, but in matters of relationships are actually quite naive; talk of being in love, but are actually merely infatuated with the idea of playing grown-up love roles; talk of being liberated, but rarely even allow themselves to enjoy spontaneity. Tragically, because they cannot admit their weaknesses, these women cannot confront and grow beyond them.

At the other end of the spectrum is the "Tinker" (named for J. M. Barrie's Tinkerbell, who had no patience with Peter Pan's behavior). Tinker is a woman who is willing to grow up. She accepts her responsibility for half of a relationship and expects the same of her man, refusing to indulge his immature ways. She has the courage to confront her weaknesses and grow beyond them. Whereas a Wendy is a man's mother, a Tinker is his true companion. Wendy is caught in a trap; Tinker is not.

Many women find themselves vacillating somewhere between Wendy and Tinker. They can remember glowing moments of sharing and teamwork, yet are disheartened by their man's pouting and selfishness. They endure tantrums, hoping that maturity will eventually emerge. They mother the little boy in their misguided efforts to help him grow into a man. The woman trapped in the Wendy Dilemma never realizes that by mothering her man, she is only contributing to the deterioration of adult love.

This book is divided into two sections—"The Wendy Trap" and "Resolving the Wendy Dilemma." The first section is the evaluation. You will be guided in determining to what degree you might be caught up in the habit of mothering your man—the Wendy Trap. The second section contains recommendations. You will learn a variety of ways to take better control of your life, especially how to stop mothering your man. These recommendations are designed so that you can implement only those suggestions that are in keeping with the conclusions you reached in section one. All the recommendations are tailored to help you be a self-possessed person—in other words, to become a Tinker.

This book is for thousands of women who "don't know what to do with him anymore," and for those women who are so exasperated with their failure in love that they are considering giving up on love altogether. Their first

xii

step on the road to healthy relationships is to realize that the responsibility they must shoulder is not for their man, but for themselves. Only when they have accepted this vitally important aspect of being an adult will they truly be open to all the wonderful possibilities that exist in a relationship between a woman and a man.

PART I

POTENTIAL VICTIMS

The two main female characters in J. M. Barrie's play serve to discriminate between two types of women, one of whom is more immobilized by the Wendy Dilemma than the other. You will hear a lot about these women throughout this book.

Wendy and Tinkerbell are the two women in Peter Pan's life. Tinkerbell comes first and, in the original story, is characterized as an energetic ball of light. She has a special relationship with Peter, the full nature of which is never really made clear. Suffice it to say that Tinkerbell is Peter's companion. As I read and reread the story of Peter Pan, I gained a special admiration for Tinkerbell, seeing her as the ideal companion for a man. In my own playful way, I saw her as my "Tinker."

Wendy is a real live girl, the only daughter of George and Mary Darling. Peter lures her (along

1

with her two brothers, Michael and John) to Never-Never Land with the promise of never-ending excitement and everlasting youthfulness. Wendy sees Peter as a playmate who might become her boyfriend. Peter sees Wendy as a mother figure and wants her to come to Never-Never Land to be mother to him and other boys in the lost legion. Because she is experiencing problems at home, Wendy is ready and willing to fly away.

Wendy's sojourn in Never-Never Land is anything but exciting. She is shot with an arrow before she even lands. She magically recovers, only to have a small, confining house built around her while she recuperates. A short time later, she finds herself living in a tree stump, playing nursemaid to several undisciplined little boys, and being badgered into assuming a mother role by the fellow she wants to love. What she had hoped would be a dream turns out to be a nightmare.

Wendy's complaints are mild in light of her disappointment. She tries to resist the surrogate-mother role, but, because of her own uncertainties and Peter's single-minded insistence, she reluctantly accepts it.

Wendy masquerades as Peter's mate while, in truth, she behaves like his mother. The more she deceives herself, the more she believes the deception. She is mesmerized by a mirage that slowly becomes her reality. She is trapped. The conflicts in her life lead her in circles. The trap is made worse by the fact that she never realizes what is happening.

Tinker, on the other hand, does not permit herself

to be trapped. She flits about Never-Never Land, doing her own thing. She too, wants to be Peter's special person, but not at the price of her own freedom. Except for their affection for Peter, Wendy and Tinker are quite different.

Wendy accedes to Peter's whims; Tinker challenges them. Wendy permits herself to be blackmailed by the threat of Peter's tantrums; Tinker refuses to be intimidated by such foolishness. Wendy is a model of propriety and sobriety; Tinker is outspoken to a fault. Of the two, Tinker is the one who makes life move, though not always in a peaceful direction.

There is a bit of Wendy and Tinker in all women. To the degree that Wendy dominates your life, you are being pulled toward the mothering trap. To the degree that the Tinker inside you sparkles her message of freedom, you are moving away from the mothering trap, resolving the Wendy Dilemma. The better you get to know yourself, the less likely you'll be to try to play mother to the man you love.

1
One Woman Caught in the Trap

WENDY: "Oh dear, I am sure I sometimes think that spinsters are to be envied."

It wasn't her drinking, guilt, or being hospitalized that made Cindy realize she had hit bottom. Strangely enough, it was a positive experience that woke her up to the fact that she couldn't sink any lower. It happened every time her husband, Ed, went out of town on a business trip.

Cindy was embarrassed to admit it, but she looked forward to Ed's leaving. Her attitude improved as soon as he left for the airport. While he was gone, she could look forward to better sleep, more effective control of her children, and an overall drastic improvement in her outlook on life. It was this odd feeling of relief that taught Cindy that life with Ed had hit rock bottom.

"I never knew how miserable I was until the misery was gone." With this reflection, Cindy was able to gain perspective on her life, a life in which being unfulfilled was the norm.

Cindy's mother was a martyr. She was a bright

5

woman who never had a chance to grow beyond the housewife role. Though disappointed with her lot in life, she didn't dare complain about it. She was held prisoner by the fear of rejection. Her only solace was that offered by the identity of self-sacrifice. She wore her martyrdom as a badge of honor. Unknowingly, she passed these traits on to her daughter.

The fear of not being able to love was an addendum to Cindy's fear of rejection. By the time she met and married Ed, she had soured on everything. She had settled on Ed because she believed he was the best she could hope for.

She denied the fact that Ed was demanding and indifferent. She overprotected him by satisfying his every whim. Her complaints were incessant. She was jealous of his friends, not so much because they took him away from her, but because she wanted to have fun too. Her migraine headaches were a testament to her martyrdom. At bedtime, Cindy avoided Ed, thinking that depriving him of sex would somehow make her life better.

Cindy worked as secretary to the president of a bank. She was attractive and efficient, not lacking in friends or chances for extramarital romance. She had an affair with a man from the trust department, a plain-looking man with big brown eyes and a gentle touch. She tried to fall in love with him, but couldn't. He said he loved her. She didn't care.

Cindy was afraid to leave Ed, but dying inside each day she stayed. Some of her reasons for not leaving were real (money and child care), and some were irrational (her mother wouldn't like it). She tried to convince herself that there was hope that her love would come back. It was difficult for her to accept that she had never loved Ed.

She summed up her dilemma this way: "I wish he'd beat me, or run off with another woman—anything to make my decision easier. But he's not a bad man, and I don't hate him. He just never grew up. I guess I haven't either."

Cindy found it difficult to believe that her problems went beyond her marriage. It was easy to trace her troubles back to Ed. He was an insensitive lover, more of a hindrance than a help with the children, and he was never there when she needed a shoulder to cry on. It wasn't preposterous for her to believe that her troubles would disappear if she found the right man.

"If the 'right' man walked up to you today and swept you up in his arms, you would make a mess of things within a month," I told her during one of our sessions.

Cindy looked as if I had just stolen her favorite doll.

"How can you say that?"

"I say that because your trouble with Ed is only the foliage in the trees, not the roots. It's only the symptom, not the disease. The cause of your problems is not a man; it's you. As long as you try to solve your problems by finding a man, you'll just chase your tail, ending up back where you started."

Cindy was caught in the Wendy trap. She was at the bottom of a pit, going around in circles, surrounded by the voices of confusion.

The voices came from within her, posing questions that seemed unanswerable. If we could have gotten inside her head, here is what we would have heard:

When he's cruel to me, why do *I* feel guilty?
Why do things always go his way?
Why can't I say no and stick to it?
Why can't I depend upon him?
Why do I always end up wanting to yell at him as if he were one of my kids?
Why do I feel like his mother?
If he keeps this up, what will I do with him?
Why can't I make him change?
Why does he like to see me suffer?
Why can't he love me the way I love him?
What did I do to deserve this?
What would he do if he didn't have me to take care of him?

These are the questions that create the Wendy Dilemma. As a woman struggles to answer them, more general questions arise, their answers even more elusive.

Why do I allow myself to sink to his level?
Why has "falling in love" put me in such misery?
Why are all men so cruel?
Why does he get so mad at me when I do something wrong?
Why do I even stay with him?

Why don't I learn to shut my mouth?

Why do I need him so badly?

Why does he have a wall that keeps me out?

Why do I want to blame my mother for my love troubles?

Couldn't I have spotted these problems sooner?

Why do I seem to threaten him?

What if he won't change? I could never divorce him.

This book will answer these questions. If you read carefully, not only will you understand the answers, but you'll also realize why the questions are asked in the first place. With these two insights, you'll be prepared to resolve the Wendy Dilemma and escape or avoid the Wendy trap.

2

Are You in Danger of the Wendy Trap? A Test

WENDY: "Well, good-bye, Peter; and remember not to bite your nails."

All women mother their man sometimes, even if only to offer him words of pity when he's had a rough day. You needn't worry about this sort of incidental mothering; it won't destroy your relationship. The question is not *whether* you mother your man, but *how often* and *whether you're aware of it*. Remember, women fall into the Wendy trap without realizing it.

THE WENDY TEST

The following test permits you to evaluate the extent to which you are in danger of falling into the Wendy trap. It calls for you to take a survey of your thoughts, feelings, and behavior. By identifying the inappropriate mothering in your daily behavior, it will point you in the direction of change.

10

It's a good idea to take this test in private, writing down your answers for future reference. Then, have the man in your life take the test as *he sees you.* Comparing your answers with his can open the door to constructive discussion. If you are "unattached," refer back to your last relationship in responding to any question about the man in your life. Don't be embarrassed to find some Wendy in you — there's a bit of Wendy in all women, just as there is a bit of Peter Pan in all men. This gives us something to share and work on together.

Read each of the statements below and decide whether or not it applies to you. If it doesn't, give the statement a score of 0. If it does, decide whether it applies sometimes (a score of 1), or almost always (a score of 2). The "he" or "him" refers to the man in your life.

Look at this test as an opportunity to review your behavior, not as a process of diagnosing a "disease." It is intended to stimulate honest self-evaluation and an improved relationship.

0 1 2 When he needs attention, I give it to him, but I never seem to get it in return.

0 1 2 I must watch my words for fear of saying something that might offend him.

0 1 2 He never lets me win an argument.

0 1 2 I am jealous of his friends. They're more important to him than I am.

0 1 2 I feel that he doesn't give me the freedom to do what I want.

0 1 2 I get upset when plans change.

0 1 2   I blame my mother for many of my problems.

0 1 2   When he is insensitive to me, I think, "What did I do to deserve this?"

0 1 2   I would like to hug my father (or, if he's deceased, I used to want to), but I'd feel (would have felt) funny if I tried.

0 1 2   When we have a fight, I remind him in detail of a mistake he made a long time ago.

0 1 2   I wish our relationship were better, but I can't do anything about it.

0 1 2   When he's late, I quiz him as to his whereabouts.

0 1 2   I have a very difficult time making up my mind; I rely on friends to help me make a decision.

0 1 2   I complain to him that he doesn't share his feelings with me.

0 1 2   I hardly ever enjoy sex.

0 1 2   When I think of leaving the relationship, I think, "I couldn't make it without him" (or, "He couldn't make it without me").

0 1 2   When he criticizes me for a messy house or food he doesn't like, I feel guilty.

0 1 2   I explain to him how his parents (or his childhood) have caused his problems.

0 1 2   I make excuses for his behavior to friends and relatives.

0 1 2   He can hurt my feelings very easily.

Now add up the scores. Use the following guide to gauge the extent of your Wendy response.

0 to 7   You are most likely a Tinker. You may be a bit headstrong, but you're never dull or repetitious in the way you handle life. You control your own life and expect the people close to you to do likewise. You are constantly on the lookout for new ways to express your freedom. You realize that you cannot sustain a love relationship without spontaneity—the freedom to say whatever is on your mind. A Tinker may experience a part of the Wendy Dilemma, but she never stops growing.

8 to 25   You are most likely a Wendy-becoming-a-Tinker. Because you are in the process of resolving your conflicts, you have many characteristics of a person altering her outlook on life. You have doubt, but it is not crippling. Your move toward freedom is infectious. You push for continual change, often at the price of confusion and anxiety. You are moving in a positive direction; just remember that change usually requires one step back before you can take two steps forward.

26 to 40   You are most likely caught or very nearly caught in the Wendy trap. Chances are that the Wendy Dilemma has immobilized you. You are filled with self-doubt, easily overwhelmed by people whom you feel you must please. You feel inferior to many people and allow others to control your destiny. Your fears and insecurities force you to control your life by pleasing others. You are easily frightened, and disappointment hurts deeply— though you may pretend it doesn't. Normal, everyday strife causes you much anxiety.

If you have a low total (under 10), pay careful attention to any statement scored as "almost always." It could be a danger signal, calling for further self-examination. If you are currently "unattached," your score might be artificially low. If that is the case, concentrate on other areas of your life. (For example, do you mother your male co-workers, boss, or friends?)

In J. M. Barrie's play, Wendy eventually outgrows her need to escape to Never-Never Land. She gets married, has a child, and makes certain that her daughter feels secure, so that she doesn't have to run away. In her own way, Wendy resolves her dilemma and becomes a Tinker.

In reality, Wendy women don't grow up simply

because they grow older. If anything, they withdraw even farther into themselves, using mothering to hide their fears and insecurities.

Whatever the degree to which you are immobilized by the Wendy Dilemma, use this book as a means of recognizing and confronting these fears and insecurities. Remember—you can't begin your total transformation to Tinker until you know and understand the Wendy deep inside.

PART II

THE TRAP IS SET

Certain conditions have to exist before a woman gives away control over her life, becomes immobilized by the Wendy Dilemma, and falls into the mothering trap. She must suffer to some degree from a fear of rejection, perpetuate a negative self-image through an inner voice of inferiority, and become so dedicated to her social image that she fails to examine her true personal life. Once these conditions exist, she is enticed by the trap's bait: a Peter Pan man.

The next four chapters will help you understand how these factors set the Wendy trap—and how each must be present in order for a woman to become a victim.

3

The Fear of Rejection

WENDY: (making a last attempt): "You don't feel you would like to say anything to my parents, Peter, about a very sweet subject?"

PETER: "No, Wendy."

WENDY: "About me, Peter?"

PETER: "No." (He gets out his pipes, which she knows is a very bad sign.)

We know why Peter Pan runs away to Never-Never Land. Unable to face the pain of rejection, he says, in effect, "If growing up hurts like this, I don't want any part of it."

But why is Wendy so quick to follow Peter? And why, after realizing that she is trapped in the role of mother to Peter and the legion of lost boys, does she choose to stay? Is it a quirk in her subconscious? A result of cultural programming? Of genetic disposition? Does she enjoy playing mother to the man she wants to love? We find the answer not by looking where Wendy runs *to*, but by looking where she runs away *from*.

Wendy's father is an immature, childish man who manipulates his wife and daughter for his own selfish needs. Her mother plays along, sometimes taking the role of dutiful little girl, at other times that of the superior, take-charge mother figure. Very early in life, Wendy is forced to suppress her youthful spirit in favor of the dictates of two grown-ups who are only playing at being adults. When she has a chance to fly away, she takes it. It never occurs to her that she is jumping from the frying pan into the fire.

The trouble that afflicts Wendy and her parents can be seen in many of today's families. Adult problem solving and a spirit of unity are disappearing at the cost of unbridled narcissism. Parents are so busy grappling with their own immaturity that children are often left to grow up without rational guidance or control.

Cindy, whom we met in Chapter I, grew up in a home filled with the pretense of love. Her parents didn't divorce until she was fifteen, though they had considered it soon after they were married; they knew they weren't ready for a mature commitment. But when Cindy's mother became pregnant, the idea of divorce was out. They must stay together "for the child's sake." That was their mistake.

The necessity of enduring a boring, unfulfilling marriage combined with cultural imperatives so prevalent in the post-World War II years pushed Cindy's parents into the restrictive roles of "breadwinner" and "housewife." Though these roles inhibited growth and maturation, they were a source of self-esteem. Cindy's father took pride in earning money, and her mother found meaning in taking care of a child and a home.

They were able to maintain their balance as "grown-ups," provided each followed certain rules. Cindy's mother was not to earn any substantial amount of money, and her father was not to concern himself with household matters. His involvement in child rearing was to be defined by his wife. He was content to keep an emotional distance between himself and his family. He had been taught by his father that emotions were effeminate and, consequently, had never learned how to identify and communicate his feelings.

Cindy's parents had what might be called a "sandbox relationship." They played the game of relating much like two preschoolers play grown-up. The boundaries of power were clear, and they took turns controlling the game: "I'll play the father now, and you be my servant. Then I'll be the little boy, and you'll be the grown-up."

Each adapted to the roles without question, unable to explore the real meaning of being a person. Trading power was their way of salvaging pride out of their psychological prison.

Like all children, Cindy needed her parents' love and support. The strength of her self-concept was dependent upon experiencing feelings of comfort, security, and belonging—dependency needs that, for the most part, went unfulfilled. Her mother gave her hugs and words of praise, but they were shallow and stilted. Her father gave her virtually no message of love or warmth, beyond occasionally calling her "sweetie."

This atmosphere had a negative impact on Cindy,

especially during the first five years of her life. These are the prelanguage days; that is, a time when experiences result in conditioned learning over which a child has little or no control. Except for the normal process of learning to say no (which Cindy rarely said), and the influence of her genetic predispositions, Cindy was a passive student in her parents' home.

It's not surprising that Cindy was plagued by feelings of insecurity before she was old enough even to understand them. She felt emotionally isolated from her father and excessively dependent upon the affection "dispensed" by her mother. Eventually Cindy's insecurity, fueled by the fear of abandonment, virtually controlled her behavior. She organized her life around pleasing her parents, especially her father, whose love was most in doubt. Her fear of abandonment drove her to perform correctly, not because it made her feel good, but because she was terrified of displeasing them.

By the time she started school, Cindy's negative self-concept was firmly in place. Whenever she failed to perform according to the standards set for her, she felt like a bad little girl. When she got angry at her parents for making her go to bed, she'd feel very bad inside. What had been a fear of abandonment in her early years now became a fear of rejection. Disappointing her parents, even in her thoughts, carried the threat of losing their love.

Cindy was afraid most of the time. At the age of seven she suffered severe stomach cramps that the doctor said were probably caused by an allergy.

They were in fact a manifestation of nervous tension.

Cindy's search for self-identity was like that of all children; that is, it was egocentric—''Everything that happens is somehow caused by me.'' Sometime between the ages of seven and ten, Cindy reached the conclusion that her father didn't love her because *she wasn't lovable.* Something was wrong with her. It was at this point that Cindy worked even harder to be like her mother.

She went through a period in which she'd do anything to please her father. If she could win his love, maybe she could undo her ''badness'' and be released from her fear of rejection. She studied hard and got good grades. Her father said nothing. The only time he gave her words of praise was when Cindy helped with housework. She still remembers feeling very proud of herself for ironing his handkerchiefs.

Around the age of eleven, Cindy began having fits of anger. They weren't violent; most took the form of preadolescent back talk. Though she couldn't know that this was quite understandable, given the onset of puberty and the frustration caused by her negative self-concept, she did realize that the anger made things worse. Her father expressed his disapproval by shaking his head and saying that she wasn't being ladylike. Her mother's words cut the deepest: ''Look how you treat the people who love you!''

Cindy finally discovered why she wasn't lovable. Everytime she tried to love, she failed. She then began to view herself as an unloving person. With the heightened sensitivity of puberty came the notion that she could be happier if only she learned to do one thing: *stop trying to love people.* After all, that was what had caused her trouble in the first place. If she didn't try to love, she wouldn't end up hurting so bad.

Her entry into junior high school marked the beginning of Cindy's attempt to shut off her need to give and receive love. The reasoning made sense to her. If she never tried to give love, she need not fear rejection; hence, no hurt. As Cindy avoided love, her pain lessened. When she had become successful at not caring about what her father said or didn't say to her, she felt more kindly toward him. She even felt sorry for him. When she ironed his handkerchiefs or fixed his dinner, he'd say, "Thanks, young lady." Cindy pitied his helplessness and gave him that cold, generic smile patented by her mother.

But as Cindy dulled her emotions toward her father, she grew angry at her mother. Cindy didn't realize it at the time, but a part of her hated her mother for being so weak in her relationship to her husband. Cindy's anger toward her mother was safe. She could hate her because she sensed her ability to withstand it. However, she made a subconscious decision never to get angry with her father. In doing this, she protected herself and him. She knew that if she hated him, he would be too weak not to reject her in return. Although hidden, Cindy's early conditioning regarding abandonment was operating at full strength.

Cindy was popular in high school. She always had a steady boyfriend. It wasn't that she cared that much about going steady; she just craved the attention. She dated boys with fragile egos and knew exactly how to please them. She used oral sex as a means of avoiding intercourse. She tried to masturbate, but found it distasteful.

By the time she entered college, Cindy's fear of love and rejection was neatly buried in her subconscious. Feminism was a growing force on her college campus, and Cindy became a leader, drawn to the promise of "liberation." Little did she realize that she was in bondage to her own fears, not to the opposite sex.

Cindy had a difficult time explaining why she was so submissive toward Ed, her fiancé. She told her friends that she was just humoring him and that things would change after they were married. Although it sounded silly, Cindy really believed it.

Cindy postponed the marriage twice, saying both times that problems with her new career made the timing all wrong. When she finally got married, it was for two reasons. Publicly, she said she loved him and that it was time to settle down. Privately, she was pressured to get married by her and Ed's families, whose potential disapproval was resurrecting old fears of rejection.

It didn't take Cindy long to fall into the rut of mothering her man. It was convenient and safe, and Ed seemed quite happy being taken care of. Many of their fights centered on Cindy's job. She was making a substantial amount of money, a clear violation of the unspoken rules governing the traditional man-woman relationship. There was a lot of frustration inside Cindy, but she used her talent for detachment and denial to hide from it.

It was during her crisis that Cindy finally understood the complicated web of fear and insecurity that comprised her personality. It was painful for her to realize that her worst fear had come true—she had married a man just like her father.

When women are caught in the Wendy trap, their behavior is forever circular. They mistakenly believe that other people can ''make'' them feel secure. So when the fear of rejection stimulates insecurity, they rush to regain control over their lives by pleasing others and thereby return to safety. Their maternal instinct combines with the example set by the mother figure in their early life to yield a method of control one might call inappropriate mothering. If and when disapproval seems imminent, they work harder at control—through mothering. To the degree that this mothering proves fruitless (and it *is* fruitless), they face the threat of abandonment and rejection. Insecurity reigns supreme and the cycle is reborn.

Most women are not badly immobilized by this aspect of the Wendy trap. They are capable of juggling rejection and insecurity while carrying out many self- and family-care tasks. Likewise, there are many women who play the mothering role without experiencing Cindy's kind of childhood. Their fear of rejection developed under different circumstances.

Martha's parents had been divorced soon after she was born. Lacking in education, Martha's mother cleaned houses for a living. Martha remembers her mother as a bitter woman with a nasty temper. When Martha made the slightest mistake, her mother would yell at her or call her a name. By the time she reached puberty, Martha had an overwhelming aversion to anger. She would do anything to avoid becoming angry.

When she married Tom, Martha served him as a slave would a master. She made certain his meals were prepared exactly at 6:00 P.M. and his laundry done the day after it got dirty. If she didn't have time to take out the garbage, she would apologize for making him do "her job." Tom was a simple man who never demanded these things, but didn't try to stop them either.

Martha mothered Tom because she was deathly afraid of creating any problems out of which anger might arise. She was convinced that if she ever got angry with Tom, he would leave her. Evidently, sometime during her early years, Martha had concluded, using simplistic childhood logic, that her father had left her mother because of her mother's anger. She was bound and determined not to repeat her mother's mistake.

Kathy was a thirty-five-year-old professional woman, trying to rejoin the singles crowd after a stormy divorce. She had no trouble meeting men who wanted to go to bed with her, but she had a terrible time finding a man who would be her friend. Her bitterness cut like a razor whenever she spoke of her personal life. Her anxiety was rampant. She hated to hang around bars and go to parties. She felt more like a side of beef up for auction than a woman wanting to share her life with a man. But she couldn't stand to spend night after night alone in her apartment. Being alone created a fear that always translated into loneliness. More often than not, she'd go to a social gathering, only to become so distraught that she'd find the quickest exit, never knowing whether she was more angry with herself or the crummy hand that life had dealt her.

Kathy went to a therapist to resolve her fear of loneliness. Whenever she was asked about her childhood, she felt chilled. Careful, deliberate probing uncovered the fact that Kathy was given everything she wanted—everything *but* the one thing she craved—hugs. "They weren't the demonstrative types," she had said of her parents with a glint of wetness in her eyes. Whether or not her parents actually hugged Kathy wasn't important. The important point was *she couldn't remember being hugged.*

Being alone as an adult brought back memories of not being hugged as a child. Her childhood logic persisted: "If you're not hugged, you're being rejected." This insight helped Kathy understand why she often let herself go to bed with a man who she knew just wanted sex. Sometimes she'd do anything for a hug.

Frances was the exception to the rule. Her fear of

rejection developed in a way that runs contrary to everything that has been said to this point.

She was the youngest of three children, deeply loved by both parents. She was smart and popular, always had plenty of good friends, and seemed to skip the trauma of adolescence. That proved to be her biggest problem.

Frances remained a virgin until her wedding night. She and her well-educated, handsome husband experienced sexual ecstasy throughout their storybook honeymoon. Frances experienced bodily pleasures she never knew. Her eroticism was seductive, demanding, and powerful. Before her honeymoon, she only knew the definition of oral sex; after seven days, she was an expert.

Shortly after her honeymoon, Frances was riddled with fear. She had never faced adult responsibilities. She lacked the pride and self-confidence that come with overcoming failure. Lacking mature coping skills, Frances was convinced that, if she did something wrong, her idyllic life would collapse and her husband would leave her. By not confronting this concern, it grew into a fear of rejection. When she started withholding sex as a punishment for her husband's insensitivities, Frances knew she needed help. Because the fear of rejection had developed relatively late in her life, Frances was able to overcome it within a few months.

One last and very important thought: women can be victimized by the Wendy trap *without even being in love with a man.* They might mother their boyfriend, boss, tennis coach, teacher, or any other significant man in their life. However, it is in opening herself to the vulnerability of loving that a woman exposes herself to the greatest danger of falling into the mothering trap. Some women have an unconscious awareness of the impending trap and choose to avoid falling in love—their way of protecting themselves from rejection. Then they forever lament the fact that ''I won't let myself truly love a man.''

As we'll see in the next chapter, it is a silent voice of inferiority, so common to women in the Wendy trap, that daily reminds the Wendy woman that she is not worthy of love.

4

The Silent Voice
of Inferiority

OMNES: "What we need is just a nice motherly person."
WENDY: "Oh dear, I feel that is just exactly what I am."

Ann was twenty-four and single. Her college education, her bright, inquisitive mind, and her good work habits had landed her a job as a salesperson with a major computer manufacturer. She made enough money to rent an attractive apartment, drive a new car, and enjoy a winter vacation in the sun. Her striking appearance and tasteful clothes took the edge off her shyness. She had no trouble meeting single men; but beyond the first date, she had nothing but trouble. She had sought professional help because she was convinced that her life was jinxed.

"Whenever I get past the 'hello' stage of a relationship, something goes wrong." Her tears seemed to embarrass her. "I have this feeling that I can't do anything right. The really crazy part is that I don't have this problem on my job. It's so frustrating to be so good in one area of life and so lousy in another. I'd like to get married, but at this rate, I'll never make it."

Ann's life *was* jinxed, not by strange, alien forces, but by a force buried in her unconscious thoughts. Whenever Ann pursued someone she liked, the force spoke a message of doom: "You'll never get what you want; you don't deserve it."

In order to fight this silent voice of inferiority, Ann first had to bring it into conscious awareness. To borrow a concept from her own profession, she couldn't reprogram the message until she had retrieved it from her memory bank and displayed it as conscious thought. In other words, in order to change it, she first had to hear it.

Evaluating her recently failed relationship with Steven was a good place to start. Still fresh in her memory were a number of painful and confusing conversations. Ann and Steven hadn't exactly argued, but their attempts at meaningful communication had gone in circles.

"I'm not certain about our relationship," Steven would say. "Sometimes I want to get married; other times I think marriage would be a big mistake."

"What you really mean," Ann would say, "is that you don't love me, right?"

Steven would waver. "I didn't exactly say that. I'm just not sure you're the woman for me."

Ann would jump on this statement. "I think what you're really saying is that I'm not woman *enough* for you."

Steven was unsure of himself. That was *his* problem. But Ann's silent voice of inferiority made Steven's problem *her* problem. When he said, "I think marriage would be a mistake," she subconsciously heard, "Marrying *you* would be a mistake." When he said, "I'm not sure you're the woman for me," her inner voice told her, "Of course he's not sure. Because you're not the woman for *anyone.*"

Ann's silent voice of inferiority was also telling her things that had nothing to do with a man. "You don't deserve to be happy." "You shouldn't try to compete in a man's world." "Why can't you be happy with the way things are?" "You'll be sorry when things go wrong."

As Ann learned to listen to this silent, inner voice, she encountered increasing confusion. There now appeared to be two voices arguing with each other. When the voice of inferiority said, "You don't deserve to be happy," a faint voice of self-esteem replied, "Oh, yes, I do." Ann felt a bit bizarre listening to this civil war raging inside her head, but the more the voice of inferiority was brought into conscious awareness, the better were her chances of offsetting it with the voice of self-esteem.

This psychological civil war is a classic symptom of women immobilized by the Wendy Dilemma. The voice of self-esteem is the product of adult, rational thinking, a voice of hope that looks at the world and says, "There's every reason to believe I can become whatever I want to become." The voice of inferiority is the product of prior social conditioning—"Something's wrong with me; I can't do anything right."

The silent voice of inferiority is usually in place before adulthood. This is one of the reasons it is so difficult to hear. It is programmed at a time when a child doesn't have the perspective to understand it.

Mom said, "Don't worry about an education. Just make sure you marry a man who can support you and your children."

Dad said, "You're my special little princess. You'll never disappoint me."

Teacher said, "You shouldn't talk so loudly. Little girls don't do that sort of thing."

Aunt Sarah said, "My, what a lovely girl you are. It's wonderful how you love the kitchen."

Uncle Charlie said, "I'm glad to see that my favorite niece knows how to be a quiet little lady."

The minister said, "God has a special place in His kingdom for girls who know that their minds and bodies belong to their husbands."

The boyfriend said, "I know you really care about me, because you make sure I don't get frustrated."

The media also play a major role in this programming. The child is blitzed with audio/visual messages telling her what she likes and dislikes, from breakfast cereal to cosmetics. Moral messages are also conveyed in this programming. "Good" friends, "proper" sex, and the "right" behavior are all demonstrated in subliminal ways.

Each one of these messages defines a role for the impressionable young girl. The unspoken implication is: "If you don't follow these guidelines, you are bad and you won't be liked.'' The rejection message is clear. Separation and abandonment worry all children, who are scared into complying with the role definition. If they stray from the prescribed behavior, they risk not being loved.

Once programmed into a woman's psyche, the silent voice of inferiority manifests a characteristic that makes it an especially destructive force in a woman's life: its self-sustaining quality. How could a person permit something so destructive to continue? Eleanor's story explains it best.

Eleanor was forty years old and caught in the mothering trap. As is usually the case, Eleanor had had more than her share of discouragement and disappointment. She knew she had to make some changes. She started by seeking new friends. She joined a women's group at her church. There she met Gina, who quickly became her closest confidante.

After each meeting, Eleanor and Gina would get together over coffee to share their feelings and exchange some gossip. Gina understood Eleanor's fears and did her best to give friendly advice. But it never seemed to help. As Gina told another friend, ''Eleanor is convinced that the other women in the group don't like her. I tell her she's wrong, but she keeps finding evidence to back up her suspicions. If one of the ladies accidentally ignores her, Eleanor is positive the woman dislikes her.

''I tell her it's all in her imagination, but she just won't stop talking about it. If I don't agree with her, she gets annoyed with me. She keeps saying, 'Why don't they like me?' I tell her that she's a wonderful person and that they *do* like her. She says, 'No, they don't.' I can't make her believe me.

"It's getting to the point that I almost hate to be around her. Our talks are turning into Eleanor's complaint sessions. I don't think I can help her anymore, but I'm afraid to say anything. I don't think she wants anybody to like her."

Gina had misread Eleanor's complaints. Eleanor wanted people to like her *so badly* that her suspiciousness got the best of her. She didn't trust another person's liking her. The voice of inferiority told her that she really wasn't likable; therefore, anyone who said she liked her must be lying.

Unwittingly, Gina fell into Eleanor's trap. She gave her something that only sustains inferiority—pity.

Eleanor had learned to cope with inferiority. She soothed herself with inner words of self-pity. "Oh, poor me. Look what I have to endure. Nobody has it any worse than I do." This "mental thumbsucking" took some of the sting out of the pain of inferior feelings.

Negative self-esteem sustains itself not only because changing it calls for new attitudes and behaviors (and change is always difficult), but also because to give it up a person must get rid of self-pity. And when self-pity goes, the person loses the self-soothing that accompanies it. Throwing away a mental pacifier and facing one's fears unprotected is perhaps one of the most frightening experiences a human being can undergo. For a woman caught in the complex web of insecurities and fears that comprise the Wendy Dilemma, this task looms as nothing less than Herculean.

5

Controlling
the Social Image

WENDY: "It isn't for a lady to tell."

Women trapped by feelings of inferiority walk on eggs. They are extremely careful not to offend anyone. They are heartsick at the thought that someone might not like them. They therefore do their best to control their social image, believing that the approval of others will somehow dispel their feelings of inferiority. It has the opposite effect. Each time these women mold themselves into the image and likeness of another, their feelings of inferiority are strengthened. They are saying, in effect, "The real me is a bad person. I can't let her out."

A Wendy is a person of many faces. She can call upon the "right" reaction at the "right" time, pleasing others and thereby gaining respect. Yet others control the definition of "right." She believes that by pleasing others, she will gain self-respect. It never works.

Approval seeking is the key element in controlling one's social image. Another person's approval makes a Wendy feel good. But since the good feel-

38

ing is controlled by another person, the woman is indebted to the person whose approval she seeks. She finds it nearly impossible *not* to try to please this person.

The approval of another person has an addictive effect on the immature woman. It temporarily overrides her inner voice of inferiority, giving her a sense of security. Yet at some level of consciousness, the woman knows the truth: "The only reason I feel good about myself is that that person likes me." Because a person's likes and dislikes change, the woman realizes that her feeling of security is precarious. Soon she must seek wider approval by portraying the "right" social image.

A woman with strong feelings of inferiority has an enormous appetite for social approval. Her addictive habit of pleasing others demands a regular "fix" of it. She's so busy anticipating the next person to please that she never takes time to realize that she is actually running away from disapproval—an eminently futile task.

PSYCHOLOGICAL DISTANCE

"Psychological distance" is a concept intended to explain the perceived feeling of kinship or estrangement between two people. The closer two people feel in relation to each other, the less the psychological distance between them. Conversely, the more estrangement between two people, the greater the psychological distance. When a Wendy seeks approval, the intensity of her efforts will depend upon the psychological distance between her and the person whose approval she seeks.

If the psychological distance is great, as with the check-out clerk at the supermarket, the Wendy may not experience much of a desire to please. She may actually feel relaxed with the clerk and, sad to say, be more herself than with anyone else she encounters.

If the psychological distance is moderate, as with her tennis partner or co-worker, the woman can maintain the "right" social image with a minimum of effort. She may worry about disapproval, but will probably avoid discomfort by projecting the image that promises praise and recognition.

If the psychological distance is close, as with her husband, father, or lover, the woman will experience the highest degree of apprehension. Her tension will increase as she searches for the "right" image to portray. Her nervousness will likely cause her to say or do inappropriate things, for which she will feel that disapproval is forthcoming. She can't win. The harder she tries, the more she risks disapproval.

READING CUES

A Wendy can walk into a party and, within a few moments, "read" the cues emanating from the guests. She becomes masterful at observing non-verbal language. Stares from a handsome man mean something entirely different than those from an average-looking man or another woman. Giggles, guffaws, sneers, and their sequence and duration all carry special meaning. The woman has tailored her reactions to these cues in light of her past successes and failures at image control.

Large crowds are usually easier to deal with than small ones. With more people and more social dynamics, it is easier to find someone whose approval can be won. In a large gathering, the woman can divide the room into quadrants and get approval from one quadrant at a time. Small groups don't permit this luxury.

The experienced image controller is usually more right than wrong in her reading of social cues. However, she never knows for certain when she might be misreading a cue. Therefore, no matter what size the gathering, she is under a constant state of uncertainty.

A woman who is hypersensitive to social criticism will recognize the pecking order in any gathering. Formal groupings are easier to assess than informal ones. Her understanding of the pecking order enables her to concentrate her efforts where they have the greatest promise of reward. Once she decides to ignore someone, she does it in convincing style. If she later discovers that she misread the pecking order, she will apologize ad nauseum to a person who may never even have noticed being snubbed.

You'd think a Wendy would avoid crowds whenever possible. Just the opposite is true. She must get her approval "fix" from others and she'll push herself to the limit to get it. She'll maximize success by staying with familiar faces, where she is confident that she can read the cues, make an accurate assessment, and say or do the "right" thing at the appropriate time.

PLEASURE TACTICS

The image-conscious woman has a storehouse of pleasure tactics she can call upon to meet another's expectations. Just as a physician's diagnosis suggests a particular treatment, the Wendy's assessment of the approval potential of a gathering leads to the implementation of predesigned pleasure tactics.

A sullen man needs pity; a shy man will receive a gentle touch. The chairman's wife will be made to feel queenly through solicitous supplication. A grumpy man will get a giggle. An older, distinguished man will be paid homage.

As one can see, most pleasure tactics are reserved for men. When a Wendy seeks to please men, she's not necessarily flirting with them. More often than not, she is trying to please them, much as a daughter would try to please her father. In fact, that is exactly what she is doing.

SAYING NO STIMULATES GUILT

The woman dedicated to controlling her social image gives of herself until she is exhausted. She'll go to almost any length to avoid saying no. She is certain that a no will result in disapproval.

She'll blame another for her inability to do something. She'll invent a flimsy excuse rather than decline an invitation. She may feign illness as her reason for declining. If the invitation has come from someone whose approval she desperately wants, she may, in fact, become ill as a result of extended apprehension.

LOSS OF IDENTITY

We have seen how the push to control her social image robs the Wendy of her identity. She can take no pride in the fact that she sells herself for her next "fix" of approval. If image control is monumentally important to her, she will look in a mirror and see nothing more than a reflection of other people's demands and preferences.

The woman who has lost her identity (or never found it) will be difficult to get to know. During the courting phase of a relationship, she may put up a great front of competence and self-knowledge. But as the relationship deepens and vulnerability becomes a reality, her front may crack and her "I don't know who I am" attitude may surface. That's when her ability to control her social image will fall to pieces.

PRETENSE OF POWER

The woman who dedicates herself to controlling her social image believes that she possesses magical powers. She behaves as if she has the ability to "make" other people think a certain way. "By controlling my behavior, I have the power to gain approval and avoid disapproval. I can make people like me; more important, I can make them *not* disapprove of me."

This pretense of power is carried over from a woman's childhood. She learned to believe this irrational notion by pleasing her parents and thereby avoiding their rejection. During her early years, this unrealistic ego power helped her feel good about herself by staving off fear. In her adult years, it threatens to rob her of any chance at happiness. Thus, although it was crucial for her survival in the past, it can possibly destroy her in the present.

6

The Bait:
A Peter Pan Man

PETER: "Wendy, come with me."
WENDY: "Oh dear, I mustn't. Think of mother. Besides, I can't fly."
PETER: "I'll teach you."
WENDY: "How lovely to fly."
PETER: "Wendy, when you are sleeping in your silly bed you might be flying about with me, saying funny things to the stars. Wendy, how we should all respect you."

If some of the attitudes and behaviors outlined in the last three chapters strike close to home, you may wish to take the acid test. That is, take a hard look at yourself through the eyes of the man in your life. He may be a victim of the Peter Pan Syndrome and you may be his Wendy. If this is the case, you, too, have been lured into Never-Never Land. You have fallen for the same lies he tells himself. His empty promises are the bait. You take it because you believe that mothering will solve your own problems.

When I ask you to look at yourself through the eyes of the man you love, I'm *not* saying that somehow you are an extension of him, unable to stand as a separate entity. Rather, I'm referring to the old adage, "You can tell something about a person by the company she keeps." If you're keeping company with a Peter Pan, there's an excellent chance that, to one degree or another, you are mothering him. This does not mean that you are a passive victim of his whims. In fact, it indicates that, as you permit yourself to be in bondage to him, you are gaining a sense of control over your own life. Carefully analyzing his behavior can provide you with that glimmer of insight so necessary when you are caught in a psychological trap and don't know it.

The following ten adjectives describe the behavior of a Peter Pan. Read each description and decide whether it applies to the man in your life. Each one that does is one more piece of bait that lures you into the Wendy trap's mothering role.

Undependable

He's charming and witty at the beginning of a relationship, but as life becomes boring or taxing, he tends to disappear—just when you need him the most.

Rebellious

He sees your requests as demands and finds numerous ways to resist or rebel against them. Procrastination and forgetfulness are passive ways in which he rebels. Emotional blackmail is a more active form.

Angry

He often resorts to temper tantrums when frustrated. He almost looks for an argument in order to dump his anger. Anger often increases with alcohol consumption.

Helpless

He seems to have problems he can't cope with. Life often seems to overwhelm him, and you feel compelled to help him with problems he should be able to solve by himself.

Narcissistic

He has a difficult time thinking about people other than himself. His lack of empathy prohibits him from "putting himself in another's shoes." He doesn't understand why you get upset, nor does he try to.

Pitiful

He pouts, sulks, and otherwise exhibits a weakness that appeals directly to your mothering instincts. He complains of never having any fun, but seems unwilling to do anything other than complain about it.

Guilt-ridden

He feels regret about his relationship with his mother and father, especially the latter. While he expresses resentment toward his mother, he exhibits a special longing for closeness with his father.

Dependent

Though you often give him special consideration, he never seems to reciprocate. He'll respond to your needs, but only after you've complained about his indifference.

Manipulative

You never know for sure whether he's being honest or just saying something in order to get you to do something. He seems to be the ultimate con man.

Secretive

There's something about him that keeps bringing you back. His "little boy" side can be wonderfully playful and loving, but just when you reach out to touch that gentle part of him, it's gone. If you ask him about it, his feelings turn to stone.

If any of the above descriptions strikes a chord, you may be tied up with a Peter Pan whose failure to grow up brings out the strongest of your inappropriate-mothering behaviors. Just as a man cannot remain a victim of the Peter Pan Syndrome without having a Wendy in his life, a woman caught in the Wendy trap is most likely married to, living with, or dating a Peter Pan.

The following chapters explore the ways of inappropriate mothering—what I call the Wendy responses—in detail.

PART III

THE TRAP IS SPRUNG

A woman caught in the Wendy trap exhibits behaviors that suggest she is enacting the mothering role. I call these behaviors the Wendy responses and have grouped them into eight categories:

Denial—"These things are not happening."
Overprotection—"He can't make it without me."
Possessiveness—"I can't make it without him."
Complaining—"This has gone far enough."
Judgment—"I'll solve it by telling him what to do."
Martyrdom—"I'll solve it by sacrificing more."
Punishment—"I'll solve it by making him shape up."
Hitting bottom—"I can't solve it. I give up."

The Wendy responses tend to develop in sequence. As women become frustrated with the ineffectiveness of denial, they tend to slip into over-

51

protection. Possessiveness, complaining, judgment, martyrdom, and punishment occur in reaction to a continual search for a solution. Hitting bottom can occur at any point in the sequence.

The responses also have a concomitant nature, in that a woman can exhibit several of the responses within a given situation. For example, let's say that you and your man argue about going to a party; he wants to go and you don't. You trade nasty putdowns (verbal punishment), you nag him about not spending enough private time with you (complaining and possessiveness), and then you feel sorry for yourself (martyrdom) when you finally decide to go, pretending that you wanted to go all along (denial).

The responses have an overlapping nature. If a woman denies that her man is too demanding in sexual matters, one might say that she is also protecting him from a confrontation about his sexual attitudes. If a woman is constantly complaining about the inequities in her relationship, those complaints might easily take on the character of martyrdom.

As you study the Wendy responses, remember that this is a textbook-type analysis. Rare is the case in which one woman exhibits all the responses. I've drawn my conclusions from years of observation of many women.

Pay close attention to Chapter 14. Recognizing responses that reflect hitting bottom can be crucial to your resolution of the Wendy Dilemma. The good news about hitting bottom is that there's only one way to go from here.

7

Denial

"I don't understand why my husband is so cruel to me. He makes good money and says he loves me. But gosh, he can be so mean. I guess it's because he works so hard."

You're all familiar with the classic image of three figures, one with his hands over his ears, another with his hands over his eyes, and the third with his hands over his mouth. The caption reads, "Hear no evil, see no evil, speak no evil." If you change the word *evil* to problem, you have defined one of the most common Wendy responses, denial. "Hear no problem, see no problem, speak no problem."

Women who use denial in relating to their man are avoiding their feelings and, ultimately, missing out on a chance to change their lives. Here are some examples of how denial surfaces as a Wendy response.

A woman ignores her man's selfishness (my money, my car, my friends).

She excuses his continual temper with an alibi. ("He's upset with his mother.")

She keeps telling herself how much he loves her, even though he continues to be insensitive to her needs.

She counts herself lucky to see him, given his recreational and work schedule.

She says, "He's a great guy. He lets me do anything I want," without hearing the subordination implied in the statement.

She knows that something is wrong, but finds a way to dismiss it.

The opening quote in this chapter comes from thirty-four-year-old Sissy. She knew something was wrong. She felt the cruelty and meanness coming from her man. She looked around for a reason and finally decided that he was working too hard. It never dawned on her that he was cruel to her because there was a problem in their relationship. Maybe it was his fault, or her fault, or, most likely, both their fault. But the fault would not be determined or the problem resolved until somebody admitted there was a problem.

Sissy's husband was totally oblivious to the emotional side of their marriage. If Sissy hadn't tried to do something about their problems, he would never even have considered changing. Unfortunately, though Sissy sensed something was wrong, she used denial to block an outward admission.

Denial frustrates outsiders because a problem will appear to be self-evident, yet the person cannot see it. Denial often begins as selective oversight. Here is how the sister of a denier voiced her frustration.

"I tell my sister to face reality—her husband is a jerk. I've never liked him, mostly because of the way he treats her. But she won't admit it. I talk until

I'm blue in the face, always saying the same thing. And she always gives me the same answer. 'Everything will be fine if we just spend more time together.' Then I end up screaming at her. Gosh, she makes me so mad. For such a smart girl, she sure can be stupid.''

The denier is not crazy. True, she doesn't see reality very clearly. But it is an omission of *choice*, the result of a psychological mechanism known as blocking: ''I don't want to see it because it will hurt.'' This decision is made at a low level of conscious awareness, but it is a choice nonetheless. You might call it a decision *not* to decide.

Sissy's denial was so pervasive that it extended into a second Wendy response, overprotection. She was accustomed to being taken for granted and didn't think twice about waiting on her husband hand and foot. Quick to make excuses for her man, she even took his side when explaining why he was insensitive to her needs. You can hear the overprotection in Sissy's reaction to a confrontation about her man's cruelty.

''He doesn't really mean it. If he really knew that it hurt me, he would stop. If you knew what he's like inside, you'd understand. He doesn't like our problems being taken outside the home. He says we can handle them ourselves. He says I get too upset about little things. I'm sure he's right. He says our troubles aren't any different from anyone else's. I really shouldn't be saying anything bad about him behind his back. He's really a great guy.''

This reaction is typical of the denier. She was

fooling herself. Her heart was in the right place, and she meant well. And it's hard to find fault with someone who's just trying to get along.

But there is the contradiction. A Wendy's denial is an expression of false strength. "I'm not afraid; look at how strong, bright, and understanding I am. I'm really very grown up to be so adult about my disappointments." These are the words with which a denier avoids resolving her dependency needs.

Some psychologists call this avoidance a reaction formation—a mechanism with which a person covers a fear by going to the opposite extreme. "I'm strong, brave, and feel no pain." This reaction formation denies and disguises the inner pain. In some cases, it can lead to further complications, one of the worst being perfectionism.

When we asked the woman quoted above about her sister's perfectionistic tendencies, she replied with instant recognition.

"I'll say she's a perfectionist. Everything has to be just right, but it never really is. I swear, if I drop an ash from my cigarette in one of her ashtrays, it's almost impossible for her to sit and talk to me without cleaning the tray. You can eat off her kitchen floor, and her kids look as if they just walked out of an ad for children's clothing. It really gives me the jitters to be around her."

The denier often feels that if she works hard enough and sticks to her goal of perfection, her problems will disappear. More often than not, the greater her outward push for perfection, the greater her inner pain.

If the denial is successful, it can continue for years. Maybe even a lifetime. Many women in their late fifties and early sixties are so thorough in their denial that there is little if any hope that they will ever confront their true feelings. See how deceptive a perfected denial system can be:

"I've had a wonderful life. I've been married to the same marvelous man for over thirty-seven years. I've never complained about not being first in his life. His work is very important and he's been tremendously successful. I've never wanted for anything. I know he loves me, he doesn't have to say it. And I love him without putting any demands on him; that is true love. I've never asked for anything in return. That's what I said in my marriage vows and I've kept them to the letter. It feels good to give love; that's a woman's job."

Tears of sadness glittered in this woman's eyes as she gave testimony to the futility of unilateral love. One might have assumed that she had considerable martyrdom buried beneath her denial, but that was not the case. She had given up on expecting love in return and had used denial to cope with the hurt. She simply did not try to overcome the Wendy Dilemma.

Sissy's life was a tragic example of what can happen to a denier/overprotector when she persists along the track of selective closed-mindedness. In locking out the pain of not receiving love in return, Sissy was blocking out a pain left over from her childhood. Denial gave her the ability to block out the present along with the past.

Sissy's denial system was evidently not perfect. She was embarrassed to admit that she cried herself to sleep on many nights, not ever knowing why. She often found it difficult to get up in the morning and felt extremely guilt-ridden every time she wished her husband would be nicer to her. When asked about her life outside the home, Sissy revealed evidence of serious problems.

"I enjoy going out with the girls. I bowl, play cards, and go out for a drink or two after work. I never drink at home, just when I'm out."

She resisted probes into her drinking behavior, denying that she had a problem. It took careful confrontation to discover that she had several drinks (enough to give her a "buzzy" feeling) every time she went out with the girls. It took even further confrontation to discover that she usually went "out with the girls" four or five nights a week.

Sissy was reaching the end of her rope. Although this is a sad situation, it can force the denier to do something about her life. In too many cases, though, it increases the strength of her denial. One could say that inside the denier there is a voice of distress screaming for inner peace. This particular scream might originate deep within the unconscious process, but it is expressed in symbols that appear in everyday reality.

One denier who was hitting bottom expressed her "problem" in a symbolism that was hard to understand. Her stated fear seemed simple enough, yet the symbolism behind it belied the true cause. See if you can figure out the symbolic fear contained in her description of the "problem."

"I have a terrible time going anywhere. I get nervous just thinking about backing my car out of the garage. I calm down though to be a safe driver, but it takes a while. I'm able to get where I need to go as long as I don't have to cross any bridges or overpasses. Do you know how many bridges and overpasses there are in the world? Thousands, and I seem to need to cross them all. I can't stand them.

"When I absolutely have to drive over one, I think I'm going to faint. Sometimes I think I shouldn't even be driving at all. All I can think about is that there is nothing beneath me, holding me up.

"After I drive over a bridge, my palms are sweaty and I feel a chill up my back. It seems to take forever before I can think straight. I really ought to be hypnotized so I can get rid of this fear."

This woman wasn't really afraid of overpasses or bridges. Her fear reaction was real (sweaty palms, chills), but the cause wasn't what it appeared to be. Listen carefully to one sentence and think about it. "All I can think about is that there is nothing beneath me, holding me up."

Take the stated problem and apply it to another area of her life, her relationship with her husband. What happens? The problem now sounds much different. Deep in her mind, beneath her denial, this might be the real problem.

"All I can think about is that my husband doesn't really love me. He's not there to support me when I need him. I get afraid when I realize I don't have him holding me up.''

There are two important points to be found in this woman's symbolism. First she is missing the reality that is right in front of her. She has unresolved dependency needs and she is looking outside herself to find the answer. Second, deniers often expect a quick fix for their problems. Hypnotism is a good example of an externally controlled fix that doesn't work with symbolic fears. (Pills are another.)

Not all denial is hidden in confusing symbolism. Sometimes the conscious concern reflects a relatively clear statement of the real problem. Here's a typical problem expressed with a minimum of symbolism.

''I'm in love with a married man. He says he loves me. He's planning on getting a divorce. I know this is a very difficult time for him and he needs all the love and understanding I can give him. When things are real bad at home, he comes and stays with me. But as soon as things start to look good for him, he goes home to his wife. That really hurts. I feel like I'm being used. And I don't like that feeling. I want to learn how to help him.''

This woman is denying a fairly clear fact. *The man is using her.* She is exactly correct in her assessment of his behavior. But at some level of consciousness, she is afraid to admit the truth. Her fear of losing him would probably be the first thing she admitted to if she talked to a skilled therapist. But even that's not the truth. If she faced up to her denial, she would have to admit that she is only pretending to *have* him in the first place.

Denial occurs to some degree in all women who mother their man. Many psychiatrists and psychologists believe that a majority of people use this defense mechanism to hide some unsavory truth from their conscious mind. Denial is so habitual in so many people's lives that it is taken for granted and not seen as a negative concept. One of my professors in graduate school had this to say about the popularity and treatment of denial:

"All people have a part of truth that they want to deny. As a therapist, you must gently but firmly confront the denial until the patient recognizes his or her unconscious process.

"However, if the patient steadfastly denies that he or she might be caught up in denial, then pick up your Rorschach cards and go home. You haven't got a chance."

Denial is also the first Wendy response used and the last abandoned. It has miraculous staying power (remember the sixty-year-old woman). And beyond its popularity is its simplicity: "I don't want to think about it, so I won't." When you consider, that's a rather amazing feature of the computerlike organ that sits atop our shoulders.

Denial is not only popular and simple, but it is also quite dangerous. The danger of denial lies in its apparent harmlessness. It's easy to believe that anything so simple couldn't possibly do much damage. Yet the simplicity of denying the truth can quickly develop tentacles that spread and choke the life-breath out of many significant aspects of one's life.

This denial sounds harmless enough.

"It does me no good to think about his attitude. I'm much better off if I just let him do his thing. He'll eventually get over whatever's bothering him. Pretty soon, he'll come around. I can't waste my time wondering what he'll pull next."

This woman's denial is creating a psychological distance between her and her man. If it continues unabated, she'll have to increase the strength of her denial to cope with the hurt generated by increased estrangement. If left unattended, this denial and the resulting psychological distance will escalate to the point where love is severely damaged. What might have begun as a simple act of avoidance will likely end up in a splintered relationship filled with endless accusations and grueling bitterness.

Denial is usually an absolutely unconscious process. It is not, however, always covert. Though the denier may not realize that her avoidance of the truth will result in increased problems, she may in fact hear her denial and simply not care. One might view this type of denial as militant. When this denial occurs, one wonders if love isn't already dead. Judge for yourself.

"I just don't see any future in thinking about my problems. I have my house, my kids, and he gives me his paycheck. We have a nice time once or twice a month. And when he's behaving like a spoiled child, I just send him outside or tell him to go drinking with his buddies and leave me alone. He goes and I sit home and read. It works out just fine.''

This woman's denial contains strong undercurrents of hurt and bitterness. Not only is she denying the way her man treats her, but she's also trying to hide from her own pain. She is a prime candidate for an extramarital affair. If she finds a man who shows her the beauty of loving and caring, she will probably leave her husband without looking back.

8

Overprotection

"I really shouldn't get mad at him; he is a sweetie. But you ought to see what he does to my kitchen when he tries to fix himself something to eat. I swear, the man would starve if anything ever happened to me."

Overprotection is the most common Wendy response. It contains an element of denial, but is much more. The woman views her man's weaknesses as cute or endearing as she protects him from them. In so doing, she protects herself from facing her own weaknesses. In her confusion, she converts his childishness into reasons for her being indispensable.

Here are some examples of overprotective Wendy responses:

A woman makes excuses to her friends for her man's ill-mannered behavior, apologizing for his conduct.

A wife inconveniences herself so that her husband will not have to wait for dinner. She also picks up his messes without saying anything, not wanting to upset him.

A woman takes a drink away from her man at a

party. She hides special food treats so that he
won't eat them all in one sitting.

She writes him notes so that he won't forget to do
errands that are important to him (pick up his
check).

A wife goes to any lengths to make certain the
children don't "bother" their father.

There's nothing wrong with protecting your man.
Protection flows naturally from love. But when the
protection is excessive, problems are sure to develop. Listen to a woman whose statement does *not*
suggest a Wendy response.

"I love to fix his dinner, rub his back, and do
little things that make him happy. It makes me feel
good knowing that I can bring him special pleasure.
And I feel safe knowing that, when I'm sick or in a
bind, he'll do the same thing for me."

Compare and contrast that statement with this
one, from a woman who believes she is serving her
man in much the same fashion.

"When he's sick, he really needs me. He can be
such a baby. He'll moan and groan; he's so cute.
But when *I* get sick, you'd think I'd shot him. He
still expects me to get out of bed and fix his dinner.
Sometimes I think he's worse than a child."

The essential ingredient present in the first statement, but missing in the second, is reciprocation.
The first woman knows she will receive special consideration, so she is happy to serve her man. She
doesn't have to demand that he serve her in return.
The second woman is used to serving her man, but

has never been repaid in kind. The first woman is her man's trusted friend; the second woman is her man's mother.

With the foreknowledge of reciprocation, a woman who serves and protects her man is free to do so. This is reflected in the first woman's statement. She "loves" to do things for her man, and one gets the idea that he loves to return the favors. It's a pleasure for her to protect him to the best of her ability.

The second woman knows that she will probably not receive in-kind favors. There is a note of resentment in her words. Her man may say that he loves her, but he fails to show it in the little ways that count so much. If this woman were to become a complaining Wendy, she would express her displeasure at the lack of reciprocation directly to her man. If he were insensitive to her needs, he would take umbrage at her complaining. If the complaining continued, he would attempt to appease her by giving her some material item, the price of which would reflect the magnitude of her complaint. Material goods, however, are not examples of what I mean by reciprocation in kind.

All the gifts in the world don't compensate for the lack of reciprocity. A woman who accepts gifts as the "best my man can do" will be confused by the growth of resentment and bitterness within her. She might even feel guilty for not being grateful. Yet she is simply feeling a normal expectation: she wants the money from the wallet to reflect a thought from the heart. A man who sees his woman as a "pain in the butt" believes he can erase the pain from his backside by pulling out his wallet.

When reciprocity is absent, protection can easily become excessive. There is a day-and-night difference between protection and overprotection. To see it, let's consider a problem that comes up in many relationships—the man's mother.

Many men have not resolved their dependency needs for a mother figure. Ambivalence, rebelliousness, and guilt are often present in any interactions between a man and his mother. An analysis of a situation will help clarify the difference between rational protection and self-defeating overprotection. Put yourself into the picture and see which side of the fence you'd fall on.

It's New Year's Day. The phone rings and you answer it. It's your husband's widowed mother; she wants him to come right over and do her taxes. You know he wants to watch football, but you go into the family room to give him the message. His mother is waiting on the phone for an answer.

Your man bemoans the fact that his mother always interrupts him at the worst times. He points out that taxes aren't due for several months and that his mother is just worrying needlessly. You agree to give your mother-in-law a message. What will it be?

The overprotector might say something like this: "Mom, Joe is busy right now and can't come to the phone. I understand your worry. I'll come over later this afternoon and help you get started. Maybe Joe can look over our work tomorrow."

The protector might say something like: "We understand your worry, Mom. But relax, it'll be okay. Joe will call you back in a little while."

The obvious difference between the two is that the overprotector takes her man's responsibility on her own shoulders. What begins as his problem becomes hers. The protector runs interference for her man *without* taking his problem away from him. She gives him a temporary helping hand, with the implication that he will solve his problem at a later time.

Overprotection robs both parties of individuality. If a woman is forever shouldering burdens that are not hers, she loses sight of the demarcation line separating her problems from those of the man in her life. The growth of individuality through an advance in self-knowledge cannot occur when one adult is shouldering the burdens of another adult who is supposedly an integral member of a cooperative team. This is when a relationship begins to destroy both individuals involved.

This is not necessarily a one-way street. More often than not, there is a strange sense of balance that creeps into a relationship beset with overprotection. The woman overprotects her "helpless" man in certain areas, while the man overprotects his "helpless" woman in other areas. Those areas are usually defined by traditional role restrictions. "Housewife" and "breadwinner" typically define how the overprotective behavior is divided.

Listen first to a man, then to a woman, talk about their relative strengths and weaknesses.

"She can't read a map to save her life. If she ever went to a new place on the other side of the city, I shudder to think of the consequences. I might not see her for days. And she'll probably run out of gas, or else try to put gas where the oil goes. She's a sweetheart, but I just can't trust her in a car."

The woman giggles in agreement with this assessment. Later she comments on her husband's household skills.

"He tried to make dinner the other night. What a disaster! He let the hamburger grease spill over the side of the pan, started a fire, and burned up two of my best dish towels putting it out. Then he used an SOS pad on my Teflon grill and destroyed it. I don't think I'll ever complain about his watching football again. At least it keeps my kitchen safe."

The man chuckled in agreement over his wife's assessment of his "inadequacy."

This couple had a great investment in maintaining a balance of power through mutual stupidity. The woman gained a sense of self-worth and control over her life by protecting her man from his inability to care for himself in a "woman's world." The man's self-respect as a husband was expressed in his ability to protect his wife from failure in a "man's world." Each, of course, had the capacity to learn survival skills in the other's area. Hence, their protection was excessive and stood in the way of further growth in their relationship. Most disturbing was the way they laughed about their mutual immaturity.

Behind overprotection there is always the implication of weakness. "He can't; therefore, I have to" is the affirmation that the woman makes in supporting her own servitude. But this is an irrational conclusion based on inability, when unwillingness is actually the case.

One woman pointed out how the little things trapped her.

"It started out before we were married. I would make sure he had money in his wallet. It was no big thing. He appreciated it and I was happy to do it. Then I started reminding him to call his mother every Sunday. That, too, seemed to be no big deal. It took a conversation with his mother before it dawned on me what was happening. We were talking about how Sam would forget his head if it weren't attached. She said, 'Poor Sammy always needed someone to take care of him. I'm so glad I don't have to do it anymore.' After I hung up the phone, I had two reactions. I was thankful to Sam's mother for waking me up; at the same time, I was disgusted with her for making her son so dependent upon a woman."

The Wendy finds a strange sense of consolation in her man's weakness. It makes her feel needed, and being needed is a tonic for her feelings of rejection and inferiority. If she has negative feelings about herself, she's willing to pay any price for a sense of belonging. On any one day, this price doesn't seem excessive. But as the price increases, it eventually reaches a point where its payment is more than she can handle.

Listen to a true story of how simple, unobtrusive

overprotection reached the point where a woman feared for her life. Locate the points in the story at which this woman could and should have seen the trap coming.

Betty was a thirty-eight-year-old woman in love with a thirty-four-year-old Peter Pan. They had lived together for two years, but because of Todd's immaturity and excessive drinking, Betty had decided that they should split up for a few months. After whining about being kicked out of his home and threatening to get even with her, Todd returned to his mother's house (he had never changed his address on his driver's license or checkbook). Things seemed to calm down, so Betty and he began dating again.

Before one of their dates, Betty asked Todd to come over early to help with some broken plumbing in her house, but he didn't show up when he had said he would. When he called later, he responded to her questions about his whereabouts by saying, "Well, you told me to learn to relax. So, when I was having fun at my buddy's house, I was so relaxed that I decided not to worry about your plumbing." When he realized that Betty was angry, he began apologizing in his familiar baby voice, a mixture of high-pitched whining and silly syllables put on the ends of words. "Todd-icum is wer-ry sorrio for upsetting Betty-poo." This always made Betty giggle, as it was a sign that her complaining would bring no disapproval from Todd.

Todd was still in his childish mood when he arrived at the door with three bottles of wine, as a peace offering. When Betty reminded him that she didn't drink wine, Todd replied, "Gollygee whiz, oh, silly me. Todd-icum forgot."

As Betty finished dressing for dinner, Todd clung to her, professing his sorrow in his silly manner. He put his head on her shoulder and said, "You gotta forgive Todd-icum."

Betty was growing impatient with Todd's silliness and kept telling him she wasn't mad anymore. She just wanted to have a nice dinner. As was standard practice, Todd asked her where she wanted to go, and Betty selected a place. On the way there, Todd grew progressively more sullen. She tried to engage him in lively conversation, but he wanted to talk about values, morals, and philosophy. Betty wanted to avoid that kind of conversation, because whenever Todd was looking for an argument, he'd steer the conversation in the direction of some subjective topic. The result was always disagreement and tantrums.

By the time they were seated in the restaurant, Todd was distressed by Betty's avoidance tactics. She thought a short visit to the ladies' room would give them both a chance to start over. When she returned, Todd was putting on his coat, looking as if he wanted to kill someone. When she asked what was wrong, he snapped, "We're getting out of here. They put a good-looking couple like us at a lousy table and don't know enough to correct their mistake." Betty's suggestion that they simply ask for a new table met with a caustic reply. "If these jerks don't know any better, then I'll be damned if I'm going to tell them.''

When Todd asked Betty where she wanted to go next, she tried to avoid answering for fear of upsetting him even more. She finally mentioned another place, but Todd started beating on the steering wheel, damning her for being so stupid. ''Those people are worse than the last place.'' His driving deteriorated as he swore at her about her insensitivity to his feelings. Without warning, he made a U-turn in the middle of a busy, four-lane street, narrowly missing an oncoming car. Betty grabbed the door handle, certain they would be hit. She pressed her lips together so that she wouldn't say anything. She thought he might hit her and possibly lose control of the car completely.

Todd continued his ranting about the way people seemed to enjoy making him suffer. Betty said nothing, afraid that one wrong word might cause an accident. After a minute's silence, she quietly suggested that they get a pizza and take it home. Todd agreed and asked if she wanted to stop at the bank on the way, as she requested earlier. Betty said, ''Sure.''

As the traffic to the drive-up window became sluggish, Todd started banging the steering wheel again. ''This is the dumbest damn bank in the world. Why the hell do you bank here? Don't you realize only jerks use this bank?'' Betty murmured, ''Let's go home,'' wishing that she were already there.

Todd backed out, just missing another car, and

raced back down the street. Suddenly he realized that he was going the wrong direction. He screamed at Betty, "You've got me so upset I don't even know what I'm doing." With that, he made another U-turn, cutting in front of a truck that had been waiting to turn. Barely missing it, he pulled into the far-right lane, blocking the path of another car. Its driver honked his horn as he slammed on his brakes. Todd screamed obscenities at him and began chasing him.

Betty genuinely feared for her life. Todd was screaming and honking his horn as he tried to run the other driver off the road. Betty believed that anything she might say would only make matters worse. She shut her eyes and prayed. God must have been listening, for she arrived home, but so shaken that she forgot all about the pizza. She changed her clothes, hoping Todd would leave. But she found him sitting on the couch. She sat down, not knowing what to say. Todd nestled up to her and said, "Todd-icum is wer-ry sor-wy he get mad." This time Betty didn't giggle.

When Betty asked me what she should have done when Todd tried to run the other driver off the road, I was at a loss for words. "It was too late to do anything. You were trapped. You did what you had to do to maximize your chances of survival. Your real problem is to learn from the situation so that you don't repeat it."

There were many clues that Betty was heading for trouble. The first was the excessive silliness.

Others were the way he blamed her for his troubles, the nastiness of his swearing, his narcissism in expecting the waitress to know that he was unhappy with the table, the number of times Betty kept quiet out of fear of upsetting him, and the way his temper took control of his mental faculties. Betty certainly felt needed, but she paid a big price for her overprotection. She finally sought help when she realized the price might well be her life.

Betty was like many overprotectors, in that she went to great lengths to avoid complaining or criticizing her man. Overprotection dictates that the woman pacify and serve without dissension. One woman, whose relationship was far less turbulent than Betty's, seemed content with her life.

"I would never think of complaining. He gives me such a good life. He works fifteen hours a day and never fails to bring me his paycheck. As long as I give him his spending money, he doesn't resent it if I buy the kids a little something extra."

This woman has a right to live her life however she sees fit. If she chooses to be her man's mommy/protector, it's not for me or any other "analyzer" to say she has problems and needs help. I don't like diagnosing problems when a person doesn't think there are any. But if there is any basis for objection to this kind of servitude, it is the example that is being taught to the children. Most of today's Wendys and Peter Pans grew up in households like this one.

Overprotection is, in the final analysis, misguided love. For all her good intentions, if a woman overprotects her man, is she not protecting herself as well? As she shields her man from reality, is she not trying to convince herself of her strength, her dedication? In effect, she is saying, "See, I'm lovable. Look how brave I am."

But she is convincing only herself. She is doing battle with the feelings of rejection and inferiority—emotional states with no reality other than that she believes they exist, powerful nevertheless. She'll need her bravery and heroism as long as she continues to overprotect her man, and until she confronts the fears that are the product of a scared little girl's mind.

9

Possessiveness

"I don't feel whole if my husband's not with me. I really hate being alone."

Women who are possessive of their men have a unique way of trying to cope with feelings of inferiority and rejection. Their behavior is motherly insofar as they do their best to keep their little boy right next to them, careful not to let him stray too far away. They will often use overprotection as one strategy in keeping their man close. After all, if he is weak and unable to take care of himself, isn't it logical that he must be kept under constant supervision?

The possessive Wendy is afraid to be alone. Silence is filled with the sounds of negative self-esteem. Because of this, she is rarely able to be alone without being lonely. She will even endure the maddening antics of a Peter Pan in order not to face loneliness. These are some of the Wendy responses associated with possessiveness:

She pushes her man for time commitments far ahead of the event. "I have to know if we are

77

going to the Christmas party. It may take me months to find the right dress.''

She won't have fun during an activity until her man joins her. "I just couldn't get excited about the picnic and the games when I knew you weren't coming.''

She feels jealous when he has fun with someone else. "You sure seemed to have a great time with your cousin. Why can't you entertain me like you do him?''

She demands that her man spend more time with her. "You absolutely have to set aside more time for us to be together. There's no way our relationship can continue if you don't.''

She asks for continual reassurance of her man's affection for her. "Call me silly, but I really need you to tell me every day how much you love me.''

One can correctly argue that there is a thin line between these examples of possessive Wendy responses and the rational expectations a mature woman (a Tinker) might have concerning the identical issues. In most cases, the distinction is a matter of emphasis and excess. Consider how a Tinker might express her needs in these areas:

"The Christmas party is a month and a half away. I'm going to buy a new dress next week and I'll need your best guess whether or not we'll be going. If you can't make it or decide later not to

go, I want you to understand that I really want
to go and I'll probably go by myself.''

"I had a great time at the picnic. But it would
have been even greater if you'd been able to
make it.''

"What joke did your cousin tell you that made
you laugh so hard? I'll have to remember it and
use it the next time you're feeling low.''

"I want to talk with you about how we can spend
more time together. Our relationship needs
some work.''

"Come over here and give me a hug, you gor-
geous devil.''

The possessive Wendy is so wrapped up in
avoiding silence that she doesn't relax enough and
enjoy the fruits of spontaneity and honesty. She
camouflages her fear of being alone by clinging to
her man. If he is running away from his own fears,
he will either reluctantly accede to her demands,
playing the role of the contented mate, or push away
in favor of his buddies, with whom he can successfully avoid his own negative self-esteem.

When trapped in possessiveness, a Wendy exhibits her own brand of narcissism. A concise definition of narcissism has several elements, including:
exaggerated self-concern, preoccupation with pos-
sessing things (me, my, mine), viewing people as
just more "things" to possess, and turning all social
situations into reflections on oneself.

A more detailed definition has been provided by
Otto Kernberg in the January 1982 *American Psy-*

chiatric Journal 's review of the topic. Narcissists, he says, live as if surrounded by a clear plastic bubble. Inside, they construct a world that fits their fancy, using reality and fantasy as it suits their whim. Rational thinking mixed with magical thinking, such that the resultant logic is difficult to comprehend. I have marveled at the thought processes of some narcissists, astounded that they can reason as they do and not hear the non sequiturs generously sprinkled through their statements.

The narcissism I've seen in the woman trapped in the Wendy Dilemma centers on the maintenance of tranquility through manipulation of her man. Sexy clothing and seductive mannerisms are only a part of this manipulation. She seeks to possess him by operating on the assumption that his male ego is so monstrous he will be a sucker for any behavior that plays to his exaggerated self-concern (often, this is more fact than fantasy). She is able to lure him into her glass bubble, where, without being aware of it, he is forced to play by her rules.

A glance through a current issue of a women's magazine gives an idea of the tools of narcissism offered to a woman who is searching for a way to avoid being alone. She is feeling unlovable, starving for affection, when along come these magical messages:

- Stretched muscles are sexy muscles.
- A certain bath gel is a skin necessity.
- A line of cosmetics lets the natural you shine through.

- A certain perfume attracts men.
- Gentlemen prefer a certain pantyhose.
- There is a kind of silk that is a woman.
- A certain shampoo shimmers.
- There is a procedure that will keep your skin from getting old.

Each of these messages contains an element of magical thinking, a key to the preservation of the narcissist's glass bubble. I have no idea what a "skin necessity" is, nor how perfume "attracts" men, silk can have a gender, a shampoo "shimmers," or cosmetics can be equated with "natural." I can't imagine a man preferring a brand of pantyhose, and I'm sure some unstretched muscles are also sexy. While these messages contain a certain contaminated logic, the idea that there is a way to grow older but not let your skin age is a downright lie.

The possessive woman attempts to organize her world around these promises, believing that she can hold onto her man if she follows the rules. If he is a Peter Pan, living in a bubble of his own, the interaction would be comical if it weren't for the tragedy involved.

Her perfume will attract him and his cologne will make her swoon. Her silk asserts her femininity and his suede oozes masculinity. Her shampoo shimmers and his aftershave glows. Her flexible muscles are just as sexy as his bulging ones. This illogical interaction could continue forever. No wonder the men and women involved in this sort of mental masturbation never truly touch one another.

A Wendy sincerely believes that she can keep her man inside her personalized glass bubble, if only she can perfect her seductive abilities. She maintains the tightest possible control over her man's time and affection, believing that, if she can corral him for an extended period of time, he will be transformed into the man she's always wanted. You can see why I put Wendy in Never-Never Land along with her Peter Pan.

Another major attribute of the Wendy who possesses her man is jealousy. Though on the surface she may have fooled herself, somewhere deep inside she knows the truth—that the possession of her man is, at best, tenuous. She is plagued by constant thoughts of impending failure. Given her insecurity, jealousy is inevitable. Listen to one woman desperately search for the reason her boyfriend is seeing another woman.

"I can't understand what he sees in her. She's been married before and has two kids. I know he doesn't like kids. Why is he doing this to me? What did I do wrong? When I ask him why he's doing this, he just says he's not sure of his feelings. I'm convinced that he doesn't love me anymore. But he says I'm jumping to conclusions. What else am I supposed to think? He sees her, and then he wants to see me. I can't stand being the second woman. But I can't stand losing him either. What am I supposed to do?"

Jealousy will haunt this woman, disturbing her

sleep, her work, her play, and everything else that is important to her. And she'll never find an answer, because she's asking the wrong question. She's grappling with feelings of rejection and inferiority, asking "What's wrong with me?" If she had a more positive self-image, she would focus on the real question, "What's wrong with our love life?" But she's convinced that he's choosing the other woman over her and she resists the implication ("I'm a bad person") with all her might. Jealousy is the result.

A married woman may also be plagued by jealousy. She will cling to her husband at a party, petrified of his glance at another woman. She will create a nightmare of possibilities if he's an hour late getting home. She becomes nervous if he's away from her and she doesn't know where he is or what he's doing. Her possessiveness will prevent any rational discussion aimed at resolving her concerns.

As she masses her resources to cope with jealousy, her personal development will suffer. She views any personal goals as an extension of her man's life. One woman described the limitations imposed by her own fears in this way.

"My husband says I shouldn't bother working because the money I make doesn't help that much. He says he's the one who should work to pay our bills. He says there's no use in my finishing college, because I'll never make enough money to justify the time and expense. I think I want to work for a while, but he says I should have a baby."

He says. He says. The woman was living her life as an appendage of her man. She was possessive and jealous, fearful that every time he walked out the door, he wouldn't come back. She extinguished any spark of individuality in herself, electing to subjugate her desires to his viewpoints, no matter how shortsighted or chauvinistic they may have been. It makes one wonder who possessed whom.

Here are some other characteristics that stem from a woman's possessiveness.

Showing Off

Any woman is proud of the man she loves, just as a man is proud of his woman. But the possessive Wendy tends to show off her man, exhibiting him like a prize bull at the county fair. She rarely goes to social functions without him, but when she does, she makes repeated references to his work, likes, dislikes, and moods. She can barely have an opinion about anything without somehow involving his thoughts or opinions.

"Harry would say that this food is lousy," might be the way she critiques a restaurant. When asked what she's doing Saturday night, she replies, "You know how Harry is; only the best. So I guess it's the country club for dinner." When a friend compliments her car, she says, "Harry would die if his wife didn't drive a Mercedes."

Repressed Sexuality

A Wendy has difficulty accepting her sexuality. Her desire to enjoy sex is often sabotaged by her feeling of inferiority.

In some cases, possessiveness becomes a way to avoid expressing repressed sexuality. An example is the woman who considers having an extramarital affair, but becomes consumed with guilt and she tries to reaffirm her marriage through possessiveness.

Possessiveness and jealousy are to be expected whenever a woman is afflicted with feelings of rejection and inferiority. If you find yourself trapped by possessive responses, ask yourself what you are afraid of. It may be difficult to identify, but it's a great place to start.

10
Complaining

"I tell him what's wrong with our marriage. I talk till I'm blue in the face, but he doesn't pay any attention to me."

We all complain about the man or woman in our life. Airing grievances is a part of living. It's even a part of a successful relationship. It's good to complain, *provided* the complaint opens the door to meaningful catharsis and/or resolution of the problem. Complaining can be the first step to healthy communication. However, this is *not* the type of complaining under present consideration.

Here are some examples of the verbal behavior that is the focus of this chapter:

A woman complains that her man doesn't share his feelings with her.

She complains that he doesn't love her.

She criticizes him for drinking too much (or for other shortcomings).

She complains that he ignores her.

She nags him about his lack of participation in their relationship.

She complains that he never helps with household chores.

The nature of a Wendy's relationship to her man is such that when she complains, her grievances fall on deaf ears. Frustrated, she restates her complaints, believing that continuous repetition will somehow increase the chances of meaningful communication. Instead, her complaining leads to fruitless arguing or sullen silences, during which bad feelings multiply geometrically. The key to understanding how complaining becomes a Wendy response is to realize that, in the Wendy trap, *complaints never work as intended*.

A woman's complaints may cause guilt feelings in her man. These feelings may cause him to change his behavior, but as he does so, he stockpiles negative feelings toward the woman. And the next time, he probably ''forgets'' all over again.

Guilt is a poor motivator. It is negative reinforcement; that is, a person performs in order to *avoid* something negative. In this case, the negative is a feeling of guilt. Research tells us that, under conditions of negative reinforcement, the subject resents being coerced into a certain behavior. In short, if a woman submits her man to negative reinforcement, he may do what she wants, but he'll be mad at her for ''making'' him do it.

For other women (e.g., Betty in Chapter 8), complaining can be an incendiary device. If not worded carefully at the proper time, their complaints can touch off an explosion of nasty words, threatening gestures, or, in the worst case, physical abuse.

It's always been difficult for me to understand why a woman whose man has a history of reacting violently to her complaints still complains (or stays with the man). If I believed in such a thing, I'd think she were exercising a death wish. I'm apt to think that such complaints have one of two intentions. It gives a woman the opportunity to be a martyr, finding self-significance in the pain she endures; or she feels some bizarre sense of justification that, by causing her man to lose control, she has somehow equaled the score. (See Chapters 13 and 14.)

For most women caught in the Wendy trap, complaining becomes a logical step in their attempt to resolve problems in their relationship. The following story provides an excellent example.

Connie married Lance shortly after they both received their master's degree in business. They went to work for different companies in the same large city. They enjoyed most of the cultural and sporting events the city offered and, with their combined salaries, were able to buy a high-rise condo in the best neighborhood.

Both Connie and Lance came from traditional families and often discussed the pros and cons of old versus new roles for men and women. They were prepared to learn new ways of relating to each other. They felt confident that their sense of adventure and mutual support would overcome any obstacle in their marriage. Most of all, they felt good about their ability to communicate. It seemed no problem was too complicated for them to work out. After all, they were bright, possessed excellent verbal skills, and loved each other very much.

It's difficult to pinpoint where the problems started. It had something to do with Lance's father dying before Lance had a chance to mend some fences. Likewise, it had to do with Connie losing both her parents within a relatively short period of time. She had always felt she had been a disappointment to them, especially her father. Though the reason was unclear, she always had the idea her father had wanted her to be a boy. She had never had the nerve to ask him about this, and now his death eliminated the possibility of uncovering the truth.

Understandably, both Connie and Lance were depressed during the sixteen months that the death of loved ones invaded their home. Unfortunately, they wouldn't give themselves the *right* to be depressed, or to have trouble communicating during these times of emotional stress. They pretended to have no problems working things through.

They didn't forgive themselves or each other for their temporary lapse in effective communication. They felt they should be able to resolve *all* disputes if they talked enough. They didn't know how to let certain problems get blown away by the winds of understanding and the confidence contained in the belief "We'll work it out next time."

Lance began to withdraw. He didn't try to communicate his feelings and seemed to ignore Connie. He found excuses to be gone in the evening. When he was home, he acted as if he lived in another world. Connie went to the opposite extreme. She talked more. Gradually her words became repetitious and caustic. Unwittingly, she began complaining.

It was little things at first, like "You never help me bring in the groceries" and "Why can't you clean up after yourself?" As the number of her complaints increased, so did their intensity. "You never talk to me anymore" and "Why do you like to see me suffer?" became standard fare at the dinner table. Lance responded with silence and indifference. When pushed to talk, he'd say, "I don't know" or "What do you want me to say?"

Both Connie and Lance were amassing bad feelings toward each other. Lance was internalizing his feelings, and Connie was taking them out on her man. Neither would confront the deterioration of their once-happy relationship.

Connie finally decided to seek help when one of her friends spoke to her about her complaining. "You never were a complainer," the friend said over lunch. "But now you seem to be turning into a bitch."

The last straw was when Connie heard herself reply, "Complaining is about the only way I can get Lance to pay attention to me anymore. If I want anything, I just have to keep complaining until I get it."

Connie and Lance had to face the fact that they both had unresolved dependency needs from their childhood. The death of their respective parents had reactivated some old disappointments and created some new ones. Lance had shut off the sounds coming from the present and was concentrating on past memories. Connie ran away from past frustrations by bullying her way through the emotions of the present. There was every reason to believe that, with some objective guidance, they could rekindle the love that was dying.

Just before she hit bottom, Connie started doing something that embodied the bitterness of her Wendy response. She started timing her complaints so that she could make Lance look bad in the eyes of their friends. She'd make a sarcastic remark about his withdrawal ("Lance can't handle the complaints of a real woman") and use a minor social error in the present to criticize him about the past. (When he dropped a potato chip and picked it up, she said, "Judy, do you want to take Lance for a week? Maybe you can teach him to pick up after himself.")

When a Wendy times her complaint in order to embarrass or belittle her man, she has slipped into the punishment response. Her desire to make things better combines with her bitterness that things are not changing and yields a verbal jab to his ego. She is using the man's desire for a positive social image as a weapon against him. If she's particularly upset, she may save her "cheap shot" until her man's best friend, or even his boss, is around.

When she uses complaints in social situations, the Wendy may reap some feelings of martyrdom. "Look what I'm putting up with. Nobody suffers the degree of pain that I do." It's also possible that the woman is afraid to complain to her man when they are alone, and so she saves her belittlements for social situations, reaping her rewards under safe conditions.

Complaints made in social settings are nothing more than the woman's attempt to make her little boy shape up. She's been unsuccessful with other forms of mothering, so she tries embarrassment. Even when she makes a joke out of it, the complaint usually still hurts.

Here's an example. Ozzie was complaining about not getting any cards during a bridge party. His wife overheard him and yelled across the room to her friend, "Ozzie's a big baby. He's always moaning about something. Just tell him to keep still. It works with my four-year-old; it should work on husbands."

I asked a man married for twenty-six years whether his wife complained about him during social gatherings. His answer was sadly revealing. "I imagine she does. At least, she sure used to. But to tell the truth, I never listen to her anymore, so I really don't know."

The most concentrated complaint session occurs when several Wendys gather for a social function. If they are old friends, the complaints are apt to flow faster than the wine. Pressure is created, and the women find themselves on a nonstop treadmill of complaining. There is a frenzy of complaints and countercomplaints, the competition rivaling that of their husbands, who are across town, trying to bang a racquetball into the next century. The excitement of the moment causes exaggerations, half-truths, and a game of oneupmanship. ("Your man came in at three A.M.? That's nothing. My man stayed out all night and then gave me a song and dance about having to take care of his best buddy!")

It's possible that a non-Wendy could get caught up in this frenzy. Since men and women never please each other all the time, it's easy to find something to complain about. It's easy to say, "My man can be such an idiot." But those of you who may have slipped into this unintentional complaint response will recall a very clear voice inside of you that added, "Yeah, and he's *my* idiot and I love him to death." The complaining Wendy response doesn't include this message of love.

Complaining can also be self-sustaining in another way. Consider how Connie worked her way into the Wendy response. She thought that two bright, well-educated people could solve all their problems with verbalizations. She did it on the job and figured it would work at home. When Lance started putting up his stone wall, Connie was disoriented. "Where am I, and what's going on?" The verbalization of her complaints may have been more important than the complaints themselves. She needed to hear herself talk, if for no other reason than to reaffirm that she was who she thought she was. Connie admitted to complaining out loud when Lance was gone. She said, "I'd just wander around the house, bitching and complaining about every little thing I could think of. If I didn't know better, I'd swear I was nuts. Actually I think I just wanted to hear somebody's voice. Connie was right. She did want to hear someone talking, a someone she felt comfortable with and trusted—herself.

Narcissism has a way of creeping into the Wendy complaints. The glass bubble analogy from the preceding chapter suggested that, when locked inside her own little world. the narcissist believes everything she thinks. When complaints reach a certain level, the Wendy starts to believe any complaint she thinks of, simply because she thought of it. This losing touch with the facts is rare, but it can occur, especially wth women who endure massive amounts of inferiority and feelings of rejection.

As you will learn in Part IV, there is a positive side to the Wendy's complaining. Whether it is the result of bitterness, narcissism, martyrdom, or punishment, there is a message in every complaint. I prefer to see it as the voice of a scared little girl trying to say something. She's saying it in code, but it's there nonetheless. Your job is to decipher that scared little girl's secret message.

11
Judgment

"My husband doesn't remember things well. He's a good guy and his heart is in the right place. But there are times when I just have to take over."

The judging Wendy and her man have a unique relationship. It operates under a set of unspoken rules that regulate the balance of power. The woman is dominant (though not necessarily bossy), and the man is passive (though not necessarily a jellyfish). They often exchange tense words without being angry. You might say that they have agreed to disagree.

The judging woman will exhibit these Wendy responses:

She will tell her man how he's feeling, tracing the history of this feeling back to before he can remember.

She will attempt to explain the meaning of his behavior to him, usually making a negative reference to some important adult in his childhood.

She will tell him what he's *really* thinking when he expresses a thought.

She will tell him to do things rather than ask him.

When she gives him directions, she'll often include simplistic instructions; for example, "Go to the third house on the left—one, two, three—and make sure the number reads 739; remember, that's 739, on the left."

The judging Wendy can be remarkably successful in her marriage. Her judgments about propriety are usually astute. Her memory for details is exacting. She can do three things at once, all of them quite well. She is a tough act to follow. If you're wondering about her competence, just ask her. She'll tell you all about it.

But this is not a superwoman, as the overprotector tends to be. She's just extremely competent. You wouldn't catch her cleaning her house at two o'clock in the morning. She'd have it finished by noon, and if it got dirty, she'd let it go till tomorrow. But neither is she a Tinker. She judges, directs, and implements all within the confines of feelings of rejection and inferiority. She's very concerned about her social image and is too often motivated by a vague sense of guilt. She's not sure what she's guilty of, but she's sure it must be something. If a woman chooses to cope with inferiority, she could do a lot worse than doing so through judging.

This woman will attach herself to a certain kind of man. He'll usually be seen as a good guy, rather shy and retiring. But he has a way of drawing the line in defense of himself if the woman gets too pushy. He asserts himself in a style reflective of passive resistance. When she becomes overbearing, he'll say, "Yes, dear," and either continue doing what he was doing or simply retreat into his favorite pastime. If the woman continues pushing, he may have a short, mild temper flareup, during which he might say, "Just calm down."

Neither party in this relationship pushes the other too far. If they have a successful relationship, each has learned when and how to back off. The wily judger reads the level of distress in her man and backs off before encouraging him to engage in covert revenge maneuvers. As pointed out above, these maneuvers are passive in nature. For example, a man who feels his woman was overly bossy in the morning may "forget" to bring home the groceries she told him to pick up; or he may call ten minutes after the guests arrive, lamenting that he will be home late from work. This is his passive way of being aggressive.

Let me share the highlights of a recent consultation session I had with a well-adjusted judger and her man. They sought my advice about their twenty year-old son, Tom, who seemed to be heading toward the Peter Pan Syndrome. I use the term "well adjusted" because this couple had stayed together for twenty-four years, learned how to manage each other's peculiarities, and seemed to be sensitive to each other's weaknesses; there was a feeling of respect in the air as they talked. Neither had any serious psychological problems. If they had not borne children, they would probably have lived a fairly contented life.

Dee started reciting her son's history before she

sat down. There was no way my note-taking skills could keep up. She read from a booklet she had been compiling. She interrupted herself several times in the opening minutes, each time referring to a certain page in my book *The Peter Pan Syndrome*. Since I felt confident that I knew the kind of problem she was describing, I concentrated my attention on the interaction between Dee and her husband, Dick.

Dick didn't say a word for fifteen minutes. However, I noticed that every once in a while he shook his head in dissent. Dee must have seen him, but she didn't pay any attention. She recounted her son's troubled past as if she'd videotaped the whole thing. Only once did Dick verbally disagree with Dee. When she said that Tom had never been arrested, Dick interrupted, ''He's been arrested twice, but she doesn't know about it.''

Dee's hesitation lasted a second or two. She continued her review of Tom's history, while I sat in wonder. This woman discovers that her son has been arrested twice, and she is so intent upon her review of history that she barely flinches! I was sure Dee would have plenty to say to Dick once they were in the car driving home. (I had noticed that when Dick made his surprise disclosure, he emitted a sheepish grin. It seemed to be an expression of fear rather than enjoyment.)

The casework review remained clinical until I asked about money. With pursed lips and eyes cast upward, she jerked her thumb toward Dick and said, ''Old moneybags here gives the kid money any time he wants it. He never spent any time with his son—which, according to your book, causes the Peter Pan Syndrome—but he gives him money.''

Dick sat stone-faced as I explained that the Peter Pan Syndrome is a complicated behavioral pattern, the causes of which were multifactored and interactive. It was evident that Dee wasn't listening to me. She interrupted my theoretical explanations with an analysis of her own. Dick interrupted her interruption. ''The doctor was trying to tell you something. Why don't you listen?''

She cut him off. ''I heard what he said.'' She was curt, but not sarcastic. ''As I was saying. Dick never really had a father, so it's no surprise that he didn't know what to do with his son. His mother was the devil incarnate''—Dick stirred in his seat but said nothing—''and I can see why he ran with the lousy friends he had; he surely had no self-respect. Just like Tommy.''

''I told you that he doesn't like to be called Tommy.'' Dick had found a point of disagreement and played it for all it was worth. Turning to me, he said, ''She's a wonderful woman, Doc, but she doesn't know everything that she thinks she knows. Tom has told me a hundred times that he hates being called Tommy.''

''He never told me that,'' said Dee.

Looking at Dee out of the corner of his eye and with a patronizing tone, Dick said, ''There are *many* things you don't know about Tom, dear. He doesn't tell you everything, you know.'' Turning his attention toward me, Dick gave me a belabored "isn't it awful what men must endure" look and said, "Mom here thinks that her son is going to tell her everything." Dick's chauvinism was showing. It didn't faze Dee for a second.

She recapitulated her analysis of how Dick's childhood had caused him to damage his son. She explained how she had quietly endured the trauma, doing the best she knew how, given the severe limitations that had been placed on her by fate. Dee was supposedly disclosing tumultuous years of pain and turmoil, but what I observed was little more than a display of histrionics.

When I commented on her dramatic flair, Dick could barely stop himself from bursting into applause. Dee explained that she was just being an honest, open person. When I said that others might be intimidated by her style, Dick's eyes widened and his head bobbed up and down. However, when I suggested that Dick might be one of those intimidated, Dee quickly dissented and Dick replied boastfully, "I still pay the bills."

Since it was still very early in the clinical relationship, my first thought—"What the hell does paying the bills have to do with what I said?"—was best kept to myself.

It was obvious that Dick and Dee had developed a system of interaction. Each knew how to punch, counterpunch, and when to pull a punch. Their emotional battles were serious, but they didn't want to hurt each other. They reminded me of two friends in junior high school who fight like cats and dogs, stopping just short of hurting each other's feelings, their relationship built on a solid foundation of mutual immaturity.

Dee, like all judging Wendys, engaged in mind reading and motive guessing. I doubt that Dick had ever been able to disclose any emotional information about himself. Desperate to share his emotional life, but frustrated at not being able to, Dee had simply taken it upon herself to construct what she thought must be the inner workings of her man's mind.

Afraid to confront himself and lacking in self-disclosure skills, Dick found it convenient to go along with Dee's mind-reading tactics. She engaged in overprotection, but only to a point. She still wanted her man to be strong, even if that strength came from her. So she told him how he felt, why he felt that way, and what he should do about it. Not wishing to be completely dominated, he found ways of asserting himself, even though they were usually reactive in nature.

I'm sure that at some time or another Dee said, "I know you're angry at your mother for being such a bitch." To which Dick would have triumphantly replied, "You're wrong on that one, honey. Try again." Dee wouldn't have been able to resist this bait. "If you're not angry at her, you should be. After the way she fed you a constant diet of ill will, you have to be angry. It must be in your subconscious." Dick would have attempted to maintain some integrity by saying, "There you go again with that mumbo-jumbo talk. You've been watching Phil Donahue again, haven't you?"

The woman who uses the judging response knows how to modify her role. She monitors herself very closely, fine-tuning her power. The directive mother-figure role dominates her actions, but she knows when to call upon the submissive little girl. She plays both roles carefully, never really knowing who she is, and too scared to find out. If you're thinking that she is masterfully deceitful, reconsider. She's just found an excellent way to cope with her fear and insecurity.

Both she and her man have. That's why it's tough to say that they need marriage counseling. They might very well profit from it, but it would take time and upset their balance of power, however precarious it might be. And many factors hang in careful balance. For instance:

Responsibility

The judging woman shoulders a heavy burden of responsibility. She carries her own problems, plus those of her husband and children. True, this exaggerated responsibility is self-imposed, but it becomes so habitual that it seems natural. Sorting out the answer to "Whose problem is this?" is so confusing and time-consuming that it seems easier for her to take the responsibility and do her best to solve the problem.

Safety

Though she gives the appearance of bravery, the Wendy judger fears for her emotional safety. Mind reading promotes that safety. She reads only what she can handle, her man's ego stopping her if she goes too far. Although it's difficult to see, there is a mutual protection system built into the relationship between a judger and her man. Each one's emotional well-being depends upon the other's ability to stop short of careless damage.

Guilt

Both members of this team are plagued by feelings of rejection and guilt. In trying to prove that she's not bad, the woman employs her mind-reading maneuver to pinpoint her man's failure. His fear of rejection has anesthetized his emotional assertiveness, so he permits her to voice his inferiority. He's so accustomed to guilt feelings that he doesn't hear half of what his woman says. She defends against her own guilt by blaming her man, and he defends against his guilt by closing his ears.

Anger

The precarious balance of power, the futility of mind reading, and the lack of true emotional warmth all contribute to anger. The man expresses his anger through passive-aggressive means, and the woman's cautious condemnation of her man releases some pent-up hostility. But, as we've seen before, these people are in a trap, in which the circularity of their actions forces them to end up back where they started. They express their anger in ways that generate more of the same.

False Self-esteem

The judging woman and her man feel proud of themselves. But the confidence is thin and fragile. It is based on their ability to enact the proper role at the right time. Even the woman's competence is not truly felt. I remember a moment in my session with Dick and Dee when I turned to Dee and said, "You know, you put on a good front, but you really feel lousy inside, don't you?" She nodded in agreement, tears in her eyes.

Dick's strength was embodied in his silence. As long as he didn't answer (or even hear) many of Dee's guilt-provokers, he was able to maintain his front of self-esteem.

Dick and Dee knew that there was not much self-esteem between them, so they were careful not to take too much from the other person. Their emotional survival depended upon mutual protection.

Coded Communication

It is amazing how the judger and her man are able to communicate their needs without candid conversations. Their ability to understand hidden meanings is astounding. However, when a gap in communication develops, it's usually a gigantic one. Without an effective feedback system, providing the opportunity for clarification of the intended message, this gap can go undetected for years (e.g., Dee didn't know that her son had been arrested twice).

Chauvinism

Dick's comment "I still pay the bills" reflected his male chauvinism. But the case of the judging Wendy response introduces another dimension to the issue of chauvinism; that is, *female chauvinism*.

The woman judger (Dee is a good example) is a female chauvinist. She lets it be known that, as a female, she has the unique and superior skills of mind reading and motive guessing. She would have one believe that being a female gives her a special ability to decipher the absolute truth about a man's inner being. When challenged (especially if a man challenges her), she reacts with a look that says, "Boy, it's amazing what women have to endure." This is a mirror image of the "isn't it awful what men must endure" look that crossed Dick's face.

Chauvinism, regardless of the sexual orientation, blocks meaningful communication, setting two people at odds. It supports a destructive power struggle that will only cease when both parties agree that neither sex is innately superior to the other.

12
Martyrdom

"Someone ought to tell me what I'm missing. I know I'm doing something wrong to make him treat me this way. I feel like I'm bleeding to death and he won't save me."

The hallmark of the Wendy responses is martyrdom. Symbolically, the martyr believes that, if she wears sackcloth and ashes, sacrificing her happiness for others, she will find some sort of emotional resurrection. When she doesn't, she rededicates herself to the cause of martyrdom, comforting herself with pity.

There are two parts to the Wendy's martyrdom: self-blaming and self-sacrifice.

SELF-BLAMING

Self-blaming is a freestanding behavior, but as a precursor to self-sacrifice, I consider it part of martyrdom. The self-blamer is constantly under self-imposed duress. Her voice of inferiority causes her to cross-examine her every thought and action, hunting for blame, no matter what the situation. She says, in effect, "I'm not a good person, so I must have done something wrong. I just have to find out what it was."

The self-blamer will:

- blame herself for being too sensitive, thinking that if she could keep her emotions under control, she would be a better person
- say, "What did I do wrong to make him treat me this way?"
- worry about saying the wrong thing for fear it might be misinterpreted by someone
- apologize for crying
- shoulder all the blame for a foul-up, even though others contributed to the problem
- blame herself in order to avoid an argument with her man

Women who blame themselves while mothering their men do so in order to find answers to relationship problems. They figure that, if they find out what they're doing wrong, they can correct it and thus resolve the dilemma. Self-blamers fault themselves so that they won't have to fault their man. They protect him from blame and themselves from fear. Although they are afraid of rejection, they may also be afraid of their man's temper. Self-blamers tend to be "attached" to more aggressive men.

Meghan was trapped in self-blaming. She had been a polite, obedient, subservient girl, well trained in beating her breast in quiet supplication. When problems started creeping into her marriage and her husband denied any responsibility, Meghan was quick to blame herself.

According to Meghan's description, Patrick, her

husband, was a demanding sort. He had never threatened her, but she felt intimidated by him. He supposedly found fault in everything his wife did. The kitchen was never clean enough, the kids were never disciplined enough, and the parties (arranged by Meghan) were never as successful as they should have been. He never lent a helping hand with these things; he just complained about them.

True to early upbringing, Meghan blamed herself without a second thought. She complained about her hypersensitivity. She condemned herself for being demanding. She felt bad that she was jealous of Patrick's outside activities. She cast aspersions on herself for the small twinges of anger over Patrick's lack of sexual foreplay. And she was forever apologizing for her complaining.

I asked, "Meghan, do you realize that you constantly cut yourself down?" Without a moment's hesitation she answered, "I'm sorry."

When Patrick accompanied Meghan to my office, I expected him to be a smooth, well-guarded man whose defenses camouflaged an insensitive nature. Instead, I found Patrick to be quite forthright. He said he was glad to be included in the session and wished he had been invited sooner. (Meghan had resisted asking him because she was convinced he'd make fun of her for suggesting such a thing.)

When the subject of his purported insensitivity arose, he was genuinely dumbfounded. I asked him to comment on Meghan's concerns: that he criticized her cleanliness standards ("I do think she needs to better organize her time."); that he didn't help with the children ("She says she doesn't want me to. I guess I don't know how to discipline them."); that he belittled her parties ("I tell her not to work so hard and worry so much about things going wrong."); that he was an inconsiderate lover ("She's never said a word to me except that she likes it.").

When asked for her reaction, Meghan immediately began apologizing for making a mountain out of a molehill. "I shouldn't have said anything. It's all my fault."

Before I could say anything, Patrick jumped in. "See, there you go again, beating yourself down. I'll try to change, but you have to tell me what you want."

Meghan turned caustic. "Lotta good that would do me."

This was the first hint of anger Meghan had shown. She tried to apologize for it, but I interrupted her. "Don't run away from your anger. There's nothing wrong with it."

"I shouldn't be angry with Patrick. He doesn't mean to say the things he does."

"It doesn't make any difference what his motivation is. You have a right to your anger and you should follow through on it. It can teach you something."

With prompting and encouragement, Meghan was able to talk about the things she didn't like in her marriage. It was a struggle for her to share them without apologizing or justifying her feelings. The least bit of anger seemed to shake her. She was afraid of it.

Meghan talked about being afraid of her father, not in a physical sense, but emotionally. "As a child, I never knew where I stood with him. He wasn't a touchy person. I don't think I ever saw him hug or kiss my mom. Whenever I sat on his lap, he seemed upset. He'd ask me if my hands were dirty, or if I had any mud on my clothes. He didn't want me playing with him. If I sat on his lap, I had to be very quiet. Even to this day, whenever I know he and mom are coming, I make sure I wash my hands and put on a clean dress. That's another thing—he didn't like jeans on girls. He made me go put on a dress before I could sit on his lap."

Meghan had learned to be exceptionally self-conscious around men. She developed a severe case of scrupulousness in an attempt to protect herself from rejection. Self-blaming was the keystone of this rigorous self-monitoring.

Meghan was typical of self-blamers. She had not, however, reached the second stage of martyrdom, self-sacrifice. The emptiness within alerted her to a problem. She had begun to experience a free-floating depression, which is often interpreted as "expected." Luckily, she did not accept the emptiness and depression as normal. Obviously, the spark of Tinker pushed her toward confronting her pain before it got worse.

Self-blamers tolerate problems they should change and create problems where none exist. For example, Meghan should have confronted Patrick about his criticism, his recreation schedule, and his insensitive lovemaking habits. She failed to resolve these problems and, meanwhile, created problems for herself by telling Patrick that he shouldn't help with the kids. Patrick, of course, participated in this situation by assenting to Meghan's folly without challenging her reasoning.

Self-blamers have more than their share of sexual trepidations. Because they are constantly berating themselves, they find it difficult to give their bodies free reign in pleasurable pursuits. More often than not, they see sex as something they "give" to a man. Afraid of the spontaneity of sexuality, they hide behind the role that they most likely learned from their mother.

The self-blaming Wendy response is successful only if supported by someone significant in the woman's environment. Although that someone is usually the woman's man, it could be her mother or her father (if she sees them regularly), a close friend, or a man she sees on a regular basis. Patrick supported Meghan's self-blaming by *not* confronting her sooner. He could have pushed to join her in therapy, asked for guidance in working with the children, and lovingly told her that her self-blaming was for the birds. In one respect, Patrick had succumbed not only to his own fears and insecurities, but also to the role model provided by his wife. She blamed herself, and maybe a part of him simply believed her.

There's another characteristic of the self-blamer that I don't think was present in Meghan. It tends to be active in advanced self-blamers, those a short step from self-sacrifice. That is, the hope that self-blaming will lead to someone saying something nice. "You shouldn't blame yourself for that. You are a wonderful person. You didn't do anything wrong."

Some people might call this "reverse psychology," wherein one goes to one extreme with the hope that it has the reverse effect. Self-blaming assumes a manipulative quality, in that the self-blamer expresses feelings of inferiority in order to gain a sense of self-worth. Meghan wasn't gaining anything from her self-blaming; that's probably why she sought help.

SELF-SACRIFICE

Self-sacrifice is what makes martyrdom tick. Self-blaming is just a warm-up for the real thing. I can't hope to do justice to martyrdom in one chapter. Since martyrdom afflicts a large number of people, you each have your own definition of what constitutes a martyr. We'll stay on the same wavelength if you simply add my definition to yours.

Popular opinion holds that females are far and away the champion martyrs. Just because I'm focusing on women at this time shouldn't be construed as agreement with that contention. In my twenty years of professional work, I've seen more than an isolated case or two of masculine martyrdom.

One could successfully argue that self-sacrifice is

the central Wendy response, *the* indication of inappropriate mothering. The self-sacrificing woman is expressing her unresolved childhood dependency needs, her fear of rejection, her voice of inferiority, her fear of disapproval, and her need to find some feeling of control over her environment. It is the Wendy woman's search for control *without resolving her dilemma* that breathes life into her sacrificial posture.

The woman who sacrifices herself may exhibit the following behaviors:

- she admits she's wrong even when she isn't
- she complains about all the work she has to do, but won't take steps to remedy the situation
- she paints herself into corners, knowing full well that emotional turmoil will result
- when all else fails, she gives herself pity (in extreme cases, she wanted pity in the first place)
- she puts herself in the middle of arguments or dissension, e.g., between her man and his mother
- she does her man's dirty work, e.g., returns defective merchandise
- she submits to sex when she doesn't want to
- she'll tag along with her man's friends even though he won't reciprocate

Joan was a glutton for punishment. She admitted her problems to the neighborhood's biggest gossip, wore her failures on her chest like a battle ribbon, and encouraged her busybody mother-in-law to tell her how to run her life. Her husband exhibited some of the symptoms of the Peter Pan Syndrome, but whenever he tried to confront her about her self-sacrifice, she would criticize him for failing to understand her pain.

Joan was naive. She had been overprotected by a mother who had been well-trained for martyrdom by her own mother. Joan watched as her mother took a back seat to all men and most women. Joan married when she was nineteen, believing that subservience and sacrifice was a woman's role. She felt fortunate to find a man who would support her. She was so busy being a martyr that she never realized that her husband, Hank, was willing to change.

I chose to share Joan's story with you because she was as close to a classic martyr as I have seen. My best strategy for helping Joan break free of the Wendy trap was to first aid her in identifying the major patterns of sacrificial behavior that were evident in her life. She did this by looking for situations in which she engaged in "the games martyrs play." Although her behavior was representative of serious interpersonal strategies, the concept of "games" added a dash of humor and sporting fun to her search for freedom. Here are the major "games" that we were able to identify.

"Oh, poor me."

Pity received from oneself and from friends is the fuel that keeps self-sacrifice in motion. Pity is a form of reinforcement and, as such, has the same qualities of sustaining behavior as does giving a dog a treat after it performs a trick. When someone says to you, "Oh, you poor thing. You have it so tough. Nobody has it any tougher than you do," you feel a certain sense of satisfaction. You think to yourself, "See, I knew I wasn't a bad person. I am worthwhile." Self-pity is the easiest way to receive pity, because you can give it to yourself at any time and in any dosage you desire.

After observing self-pity in young and old, mature and immature, I'm convinced that there is something natural about it. It's almost as if, somewhere in our evolutionary past, a part developed within us designed to give us comfort when we faced outrageous and overwhelming pain and discomfort. This self-soothing, biocultural factor helps us survive rough times. The child who sucks his thumb and rubs his face with a soft blanket seems to be demonstrating this factor. So does the adult who heaps pity on him or herself (I call self-pity "mental thumb sucking").

Self-pity can become maladaptive just as thumb sucking can. A little bit of pity given to oneself in the middle of an exceptionally stressful situation can be relaxing. But when a person uses pity to avoid the problem or to appease the self when the self ought to be involved in problem-solving behavior, then pity has become a problem. It delivers a false sense of security as it devours confidence and self-esteem. This creates more stress, which results in a need for more pity. Self-pity numbs motivation and robs a person of freedom. It is a psychological narcotic.

Joan had permitted self-pity to numb herself to significant areas of her life. "Oh, poor me" became the theme of her coping when the children ignored her directives, her husband was insensitive, and her friends disappointed her. Enduring heartache seemed to be her destiny. Self-pity was so habitual that Joan had a tough time hearing it. But she did recognize the fact that, when others disappointed her, she didn't confront them. She walked away, giving herself a variety of excuses. "They didn't mean it," "She's just a child," and "He's really sorry" were one-liners Joan used to convince herself that nothing could be done about the situation. However, as she was walking away, the habitual voice of self-pity was soothing her. "You poor thing, nobody cares enough to see that you're hurting. Why me? It's just not fair."

The most destructive element in self-pity is that in the self-soothing of "Oh poor me," the person says to herself, "I'm not as deserving as the next person. I'm a poor *thing.*" Once Joan heard and confronted self-pity, it led her deeper into herself, and she uncovered the destructive influence of the silent voice of inferiority.

"Yes, but . . ."

When the voice of reason confronts the habitual self-sacrificer, a standoff usually results. When I first confronted Joan about her children, our conversation sounded like this:

"Why don't you tell your kids to get moving or they'll lose the television for the rest of the night?"

"Sure, but what if they don't care?"

"Then take away something that they do want."

"Okay, but what if that doesn't work?"

"Then keep experimenting until you find something that does."

"But that will take all my time. I won't have any time left to be a mom."

"Sure you will. In fact, if you find the right combination of disciplinary strategies, you'll have *more* time to be a mom."

"Yes, but I have to have time for myself too."

Joan was hanging onto her identity for dear life. That is the major stumbling block of entrenched self-pity. Joan was afraid that if she lost self-pity, she would lose a big part of herself. "Yes, but" became Joan's central reasoning strategy. It is impossible to successfully argue with "Yes, but." A person clings to it as a defense against the fear of confronting and changing the truth. As I said to Joan and will say to any self-sacrificer whose trap includes self-pity, "You'll never get rid of self-pity until you confront the truth."

"If it weren't for . . ."

The self-sacrificer blames herself for everything that happens. This burden becomes awesome, so early in the game she blames other people whenever possible. When the extropunitive attitude is firmly in place, she feels sorry for herself for being forced to endure so many people who seem to delight in making her life miserable.

"If it weren't for those kids down the block, my kid wouldn't be so sassy. The teachers don't demand respect; how am I supposed to? The guys at the office are always womanizing, and it rubs off on my husband. If it weren't for a meddling government, the family unit would be stronger."

Such blame throwing is the direct result of a woman's belief that she has no control over the events that led up to the problem she's faced with. Feelings of rejection, inferiority, and self-pity have sapped her strength. Mothering her man and controlling her social image have taught her that control is founded in the ability to cause others to behave in a certain way. Since this is impossible, she has no control. Blame throwing is a desperate attempt to pacify the turmoil created by feelings of powerlessness.

"Cure me, betcha can't."

When a self-sacrificer goes for counseling, she often engages in a game designed to thwart help. She wants to hold onto the protection from risks and rejection, but she wants to get rid of the despair and depression. She approaches professional help with a posture that says, "Help me, but I don't want it to hurt." If the adviser confronts a sensitive issue or a topic that scares the woman, she will engage in any one of hundreds of strategies designed to say, "Cure me, betcha can't."

The logic (if you can call it that) behind "Cure me, betcha can't" goes something like this: "The way I live is very painful and I would like to change. But change is also painful *and* scary. I'll go to a counselor, and if she says anything that scares me, I'll find a reason why it won't work. If my reasoning is stronger than her advice, I can stay right where I am, secure with the knowledge that a professional person was unable to shake my behavior. Therefore, my behavior isn't as bad as I thought it was, and it should get better since it's so stable."

Joan asked for some homework assignments to help her cope with her children. Yet each time I gave her tried-and-true suggestions, she came back frustrated with failure and somewhat perturbed with me for not giving her something that worked. Although no child-rearing suggestion is 100 percent foolproof, it quickly became apparent that Joan was sabotaging every piece of advice I gave her. It was unconscious sabotage, but sabotage nonetheless.

There are many varieties of "games martyrs play." I've given you four of the major strategies employed when martyrs hang onto their attitudes as if their lives depended upon it. Despite their number, all the games contain the same lie; that is, "I'm not strong enough to confront and overcome my problems."

Once Joan recognized how self-sacrifice had invaded every significant aspect of her life, she found a humorous yet effective way of reminding herself to change. She found an old piece of felt at the bottom of her sewing basket, cut out two letters, and sewed them onto an old T-shirt, which she hung in her closet so that she would see it every morning.

She brought the T-shirt to one of her sessions. When she pulled it out, there, red on blue, were the letters *DM*. "It stands for door mat," Joan said, "something I'll never be again."

13
Punishment

"He can take me for granted, and I'll just take him."

The punisher is at war with her man. Her warring strategies are designed to release her anger in such a way as to "make" him change. But like a rebellious child, he resists the coercion, rededicating himself to trying to get free of his pretend mommy. Because she is caught in the Wendy trap, the punisher doesn't understand why her man seems to delight in his rebellion, and bitterness is her constant companion.

Here are examples of punishment as a Wendy response:

A woman screams at her man for the way he hurts her.

She spends household money out of revenge rather than need.

To his face, she compares her man negatively to another man.

She gives him disapproving looks when he acts silly.

She secretly pokes or kicks him when he commits a social indiscretion.

121

She badgers or belittles him for not having feelings.

She makes snide, degrading remarks about him in front of others.

She says no to sex in order to frustrate him.

She introduces one of his mistakes from the remote past to support her contentions during an argument.

In child-rearing circles, punishment has a bad name. That's because it's misused and abused. Punishment can be an effective educational experience for children, if it is done according to specific parameters. I like to say that there is a "reward in punishment"; that is, if it is done correctly, it doesn't have to be done very often.

There is no reward in punishment when it is done by a Wendy who is attempting to shape her man. There is no way a woman can assume the motherly role with a man, punish him, and expect the resultant interaction to resemble the behavior of two adults loving one another. In truth, it is a badly skewed image of a mother figure attempting to punish an errant little boy. Let's make some specific comparisons between standard child-rearing disciplinary strategies and how the Wendy uses them to punish her man.

Verbal Spanking

The most effective aspect of spanking is its shock value. The sudden interruption by a parent of precarious behavior provides a "startle" experience that often carries over to similar events in the future. According to my lexicon, screaming is verbal spanking.

Women who scream at their man release pent-up frustrations. If it happens once every two months, it's probably nothing more than catharsis. If it happens two or three times a week, one begins to get the idea that the screamer is attempting to resolve a problem by screaming. The punisher who screams is most likely living with a passive man. She falsely believes that screaming will motivate him to mend his ways. In truth, it only makes him feel more inadequate, thereby stimulating increased passivity.

One woman spoke of how screaming created just as much frustration as it released. "I know screaming does no good. He just stares at me with this hurt look on his face. If he says anything it's probably something like, 'Yelling won't do you any good. Why can't you talk like a civilized person?' He stays so calm that I get even madder. He doesn't even care enough to get upset."

Nonverbal Spanking

Another Wendy response is when a woman punishes her man in a nonverbal fashion. This typically takes the form of the woman spending money on things she doesn't really want. The shock value of the nonverbal spanking takes the form of a bill that comes at the end of the month. This occurs most often in middle- or upper-middle-class families in which the wife is largely dependent upon the above-average income of her husband.

The woman finds an added dimension of pleasure in sharing her covert activities with friends. One punisher explained the side benefit this way: ''We meet every other Tuesday for brunch. Some of us go shopping before we eat, others after we eat, and most of us, both. The major topic is what we bought and how it will affect our husbands. We compare reactions, seeing whose husband is the funniest. We laugh ourselves silly. Some of the girls slip the bill past their husbands, but others get caught. It doesn't make any difference. Just seeing the shock on their faces makes it worth it.''

The Evil Eye

Many mothers are able to communicate with their offspring by looking at them in a forbidding manner. A piercing stare, a slight cocking of the head, and assorted facial expressions tell the child that he had better quit what he's doing. Many grown-ups laughingly refer to this strategy as the ''evil eye.'' When a woman casts an evil eye on her man as a way of communicating her displeasure with him, she has firmly placed herself in the mothering role.

When one woman explained that she could get her man to calm down at a party by giving him the evil eye, I asked her why such a remote nonverbal sign was effective. She'd never asked herself the question.

I answered my own question. ''He had to learn

the meaning of the evil eye somewhere. I imagine that you *did not* teach him to inhibit his behavior when receiving a certain look from a woman. In fact, his mother did. And when you use the evil eye on him and he responds, what does that mean? You're his mommy and he's your bad little boy!''

Aversive Conditioning

The classical definition of aversive conditioning derives from laboratory studies with rats. When the poor rat took a wrong turn in his quest for the cheese, he received an electrical shock. That supposedly taught him *not* to make that wrong turn again.

Aversive conditioning was used in many early experiments with chimps. It was learned that, though aversive punishment helped shaped behavior, the chimps became very upset when the experimenter attempted to put them back into the cage where the experiments had taken place. In other words, aversive conditioning shaped behavior, but it created a very bad attitude about the experiment.

When a punishing woman uses aversive-conditioning procedures, she may indeed shape behavior, but her man will develop a very negative attitude toward her. In future instances, he will be on the lookout to get even with her.

The psychological zap used by the woman comes in all varieties. Each hits at the man's weakest spot. The one that seems to have universal appeal to the punisher is the "party zap." A party hostess summarized this party zapper's behavior.

"I don't think I want her at my next party. She must be the meanest woman alive. Last Saturday we had a small, intimate dinner party. After one drink, she started on him. No matter what came up, she found a way to turn the conversation to poor old Harry.

"Someone said something about the tennis tournament, and she said, 'I'm not good enough for Harry to play with. He still thinks he's eighteen. But spend a night with him, and you'll see he isn't.'

"Then later on we were relaxing in the living room and I mentioned that we girls should go for lunch next week. Without missing a beat, she said, 'I suppose Harry will throw a fit if I go out and enjoy myself. He can't stand it if I enjoy myself.' And she said all this with Harry sitting right there."

The zap will probably occur in mixed social company and, more often than not, have overtones of sexual dysfunction. The woman will pay for these remarks at a later time, most likely through passive-aggressive activities by her man.

An example of a zap executed in private is when a woman makes a negative comparison between her man and another man. This might be done indirectly: "Did you see how that suit fit Bill? I wish more men would control their fat stomachs." Or directly: "Why can't you be attentive to me the way Bill is to his wife?" Notice the form the zap takes. The criticism is blunted by the docility of a question. In many cases, this covert procedure dulls the man's reaction. He gets so caught up in trying to answer the question (which isn't really a question) that he fails to confront the zap contained in the query.

Denial of Privileges

Depriving a child of TV, music, treats, or telephone calls can be an effective shaper of behavior. The child will often conform to expectations in order to win back the suspended privileges.

When a woman mothers her man, she is faced with the problem of finding something that is important to her man and yet is within her control. Some women control their man's spending money or the availability of food, but most men aren't so dependent upon their woman that food and money will force them to submit to her directives. Inevitably, women who are looking for something to withhold from their man settle on sex.

When a woman decides to use sex as an instrument of control, she has ensured the growth of disruption and bad feelings. She has also made clear her feelings about her body. It is a tool, devoid of desire and warmth, to be used in covert activities in a war for supremacy.

If her dangling of the sexual carrot is successful, several things will happen to her man: he will rededicate himself to manipulation of his woman through clandestine activities; in an attempt to salve his ego, he will deepen his belief in chauvinism; his anger will be strengthened, as will its expression; and he will be more likely to have an affair, not so much in search of sex as in pursuit of someone to dominate, proving that he can be free of his surrogate mother.

At the other end of the dangling carrot, a different kind of deterioration is occurring: the woman's hollow view of herself as a sexual creature is confirmed; her ability to enjoy sex is decreased; her restlessness and longing are increased, as is her anger; and her bitterness toward life is focused on her man and, in some cases, on men in general, locking her into a pessimistic view of love.

The Wendy caught in this sexual trap is a prime candidate for an outside affair. Her lust is most likely buried beneath guilt and inferiority. She is aware of her need for warmth, caring, and hugging. If she finds a man who will give her this level of warmth, she will likely explore deeper into herself as a sexual person. If and when she discovers the power of her own passion, she will long to be a woman, not a mother, to a man. She can no longer pretend to enjoy sex or be proud of herself for manipulating her man. She will push for changes with her man. If she and her man work together, she has a chance to break the cycle. If they don't, she will leave and hunt for a man who can give her what she wants.

The bitterness that drives a woman to punish a man she once loved lies deep in her psyche. It doesn't evaporate in the steam created by a romp in bed or in a titillating line or two from a sex therapist. Sex is a cortical experience (80 percent of sex occurs above your shoulders). If a woman wants to enjoy her body, she had better get her head right.

Identifying, controlling, and eventually ridding herself of bitterness is the first step to the ecstasy promised by the purveyors of quick-fix sex therapy.

When a woman whose bitterness has been expressed in the punishment of her man decides to change, she must proceed very carefully. Bitterness is an embarrassing and confusing emotion. It is natural for a woman to wish it away in the wink of an eye. Since the Wendy is good at fooling herself, it's practically second nature for her to pretend that the bitterness is gone. She'll cover her bitterness with mature words (Tinker responses) and grown-up gestures. Let's look at one such woman through the eyes of her best friend.

"My girl friend has a lousy marriage. She's denied it for years. Recently she's taken a new approach. She says, 'I don't care what he does. I can't save him. I can only save myself.'

"When she talks this way, I can tell she's really mad at him. I don't think she believes her own words. You can tell that when you see them together. Whenever he says something, she oozes this sticky sweetness. For example, the other day over lunch, he mentioned something about fixing the light in the hallway. In this sickening tone, she said, 'Now dear, you know that you can't fix things; don't pretend.'

"If she really meant what she said, she wouldn't *have* to say something so nasty. She can't even ignore him when he acts silly. He gets under her skin and she pretends he doesn't. I'll tell you one thing, it'll never last."

The Wendy response of punishment is the result of extensive complaining, self-pity, anger turned outward, and a last gasp of hope for change. As always, the woman won't realize that she is caught in a trap. She may be aware of a strange sense of power whenever she's able to wreak revenge on her man. But as soon as the power subsides, she is left with feelings of embarrassment and shame.

The punishing woman convinces herself that her punitive style is the result of wisdom and worldliness. "No man is going to take advantage of me. If he wants sex, he better believe that I'm not going to give it away." This woman is self-possessed and wily in the ways of the world, right? Wrong. This woman has covered her feelings of inferiority and loneliness with a line straight out of the Male Macho Handbook. By lying to herself about her unmet needs, she has opened herself up to the same old mistake. She will be so desperate for warmth and affection that she'll be a sucker for a quick trip to Never-Never Land with the next smooth-talking, sharp-looking guy. She won't give it away; it will be stolen.

14

Hitting Bottom: When Mothering Hasn't Worked

"I've got nothing left to give. I'm numb. I feel like he wins."

As indicated earlier, hitting bottom is a special Wendy response. It occurs when the woman's coping strategies are exhausted. When a woman finally realizes that her mothering role isn't working, she hits bottom. There is a silver lining to the pain and heartache contained in hitting bottom; that is, the woman is provided with the opportunity to recognize that she's immobilized by the Wendy Dilemma. Hitting bottom can be the first step to constructive change, *provided the woman understands the dynamics of the door that leads out of the Wendy trap.*

The woman who hits bottom exhibits behavior that summarizes her life. The behavior is contradictory, depressive, perplexing, and disordered. To make sense out of it, she often must review her entire life. She may have to go back to her childhood, not for the purpose of digging up old memories long since put to rest, but to unveil the hidden meanings in her daily behavior; behavior that is filled with coded messages, activated each day as history repeats itself.

In most cases, a woman's plunge to the bottom began long before she met an adult male. Her ego was built upon the shaky ground of self-rejection, inferiority, and a push to always please others. Meeting a man who needed her was both her boon and her bane. His immaturity gave her the chance to experience self-worth via her mothering role, whereas his need to control protected the scared little girl hidden within her.

Let's revisit Cindy (Chapter 1). If you'll recall, she was the woman who hit bottom when she realized that she looked forward to her husband leaving town on a business trip. Cindy, thirty-seven years old, has three kids and an entire life ahead of her. Yet she doesn't care much about living. She's not suicidal—not yet, anyway. I met her soon after she'd been released from the hospital, where she'd undergone a battery of tests to pinpoint her depression. The tests had all been negative. Her doctor said it must be nerves. Running away from rejection and disapproval had finally taken its toll.

"Your marital problem is just the tip of the iceberg," I said. "You must look beneath the surface and search for the cause of the problem."

Cindy gave my thoughts careful consideration. "But where do I find the cause of my problems? I can't go back into my childhood; I don't remember anything much before the age of six or seven."

"First thing you do is not push yourself so hard. Start relaxing and letting go of your tension."

"How will that help me get myself off the bottom?"

I explained. "Well, how did you know that you were miserable with Ed? You relaxed when he left, right? And you realized that this relaxed feeling was very different from the feelings you had most of the time. It was the relaxed feeling that permitted you to gain the perspective. You were calm long enough to think clearly. And then, you knew. All I'm saying is to follow that same path in discovering how to get yourself off the bottom."

"Are you saying that I should trust myself?"

"Exactly."

"But I don't know how."

"Do you trust yourself to go to an exercise class? To the library? To get a babysitter and go to a movie with a friend or by yourself? To go out after work for a drink?" I hesitated after each question to give her a chance to follow me. "These things will permit you to forget about your troubles for a while. To unwind and entertain yourself."

"But that's being self-centered." She said it as though there was nothing more to be said.

My response surprised her. "That's absolutely correct. If you are self-centered, then you take care of yourself. That's something you haven't been doing very well lately."

"I don't know how to do it at all."

"Then it's time you learned."

Cindy seemed positive about returning to therapy. She asked for "homework assignments," but I suggested we wait. She needed to learn to relax and trust herself before working on specific areas of change. If she moved too quickly, she ran the risk of encountering failure and thereby reinforcing her pessimistic attitude toward life.

As long as she didn't deny the reality of her Wendy trap, time would have a positive effect on Cindy. It would help her put her awakening into proper perspective. Cindy's realization that she was more at peace when Ed was gone for a few days was a "something-snapped" experience. It may have happened while she was folding clothes, fixing lunch for the kids, or walking upstairs to take a shower. Something snapped inside her head. Some women say, "The light suddenly went on," whereas others describe it as a thought that is just *there,* and they know it's true. It can also be the "last straw" type of experience. But without exception, there is a positive aspect to the sudden burst of insight. Out of all the confusion, there is one thing that is perfectly clear.

The something-snapped experience will lead the woman to greater understanding of her life if she accepts it without fear or regret. It provides a foundation upon which she can build other bits and pieces of reality. It will even help her discover the way out of the mothering trap.

At our next session, Cindy seemed bursting at the seams with new insights. "My life is like a book. I have pages covering everything I say or do. There are chapters in my book, each with its own heading.

The headings are things I say to make myself feel better. These things work for a while. You know, I even say these things out loud. It's really strange to listen to yourself talk. I swear, my kids must think I'm nuts. I've been talking to myself all week. Is that normal?''

I purposely ignored her question. I knew it would come back again. ''What are the chapter headings in the book of your life?''

''Well, I don't know what order they're in, but one of the biggest is 'Everything will be all right.' I say this when I'm feeling lousy and everything is going wrong. It gives me a little boost. But the positive effect wears off as soon as I realize that nothing has changed. Things are just repeating themselves. Everything is not going to be all right unless I change it.''

''Sounds like what you really need is someone to hug you.''

Cindy looked away, embarrassed by the tears in her eyes. ''Yes, but I can't ask for it.''

''Why not?''

''I don't know how.''

''Maybe you don't think you deserve it.''

She reached for a tissue and said, ''You know, that's really dumb. I mean, here I am, a grown-up, and I don't think I deserve a hug.''

I lifted my voice and said, ''Tell you what, we'll review the chapters of your life if you don't call yourself things like 'dumb.' Deal?''

She laughed and continued. ''Another one of my chapters is called 'It'll all work out.' I use this one after going through a horrible argument with Ed. I scream and yell at him, accuse him of awful things, and then, when he walks away, I say, 'Relax, it'll all work out.' But just like the other chapter, nothing is changing. It's *not* working out.''

''What is 'it'?''

''Oh, Ed's lack of warmth and tenderness, our lousy sex life, the children's demanding, my unhappiness—you name it.''

''Neither of those chapter headings are bad. Once you make some changes in your life, you may need them. Let's not throw them away just yet.''

''How about this one—'Be thankful for what you have'? I use it to help me forget about the things that are going wrong in my life.''

''Sounds like denial of the truth.''

''It is.''

''It also sounds like the beginning of a chapter that says you don't have a right to expect happiness from life. You're supposed to be content with a man who considers a paycheck the sum total of his responsibility to his family?''

''But I should be thankful for what I've got. Remember, I told you that Ed is not a bad man. He tries to be good to me. It's just not enough.''

''Okay. Be thankful for what you have. But distinguish it from what you want.''

''That's the problem. I don't *know* what I want.''

''Then how do you know that you don't want Ed?''

''I don't.'' Cindy was frustrated. ''We seem to

be going in circles. Maybe I just ought to quit trying to figure it out."

I kept pushing. "Is that what you do when you run into a circle with Ed—quit?"

"No. I use the heading from my favorite chapter, 'Don't make waves.' I don't seem to have any troubles when I don't make waves. And every time I make waves, I get myself confused or upset. It may be the cheater's way out, but it's easier."

I gave her a reproachful smile. "Did you just call yourself a cheater?"

Like a six-year-old caught with her hand in the cookie jar, Cindy answered, "Who, me? Not me."

The silence refreshed us both.

I picked up the last thought. "When you avoid 'making waves,' you are acting like a permissive mother who doesn't want to confront her little boy's possible temper tantrum. But you open yourself to disrespect and blackmail. Maybe you shouldn't calm the waters of discontent. Maybe you ought to leave them alone and see what kind of a storm blows up."

Cindy paused, collecting her courage, and then confronted me with something that had obviously been on her mind. "When I come in to see you, I feel as if you beat up on me."

I was intrigued. "Beat up on you?"

"Yes. It feels like you have me in a corner and you're pounding on me. You won't let up on me."

"How do I do that?"

"You challenge me, go after me. Sometimes I can hardly breathe."

"Does it hurt?"

"Yes. Well, not really. You take away all my defenses. And that hurts, but it feels good at the same time. Does that make any sense?"

"Sure."

"I get so mad at you I can't see straight. I'd like to throw my coffee cup at you, walk out of here, and never look back."

"Why don't you?"

"Because you can help me get rid of these feelings."

"What feelings?"

"C'mon, you know. Fear, bitterness, anger, guilt. You know."

"I never said I'd help you get rid of those feelings."

Cindy was upset. "But that's why I'm here. I want those feelings to go away. I want to feel like I'm supposed to feel."

"How's that?"

She was getting impatient. "Happy, contented. You call it being a Tinker. I want to get rid of Wendy and be a Tinker."

I was deadly serious. "You'll never make it with that attitude."

"What attitude?"

"The attitude that says you want to get rid of bad feelings."

"What's wrong with that attitude?"

I softened my voice and slowed my speech. I wanted her to fully comprehend the key to escaping her trap. "The attitude is wrong because *there's no such thing as a bad feeling.* If there were, then *you would be bad* because you had a certain feeling. And if you were bad, then there would be no reason to try to change, because you couldn't do it.''

''Hold on a second.'' Like all women caught in the Wendy trap, Cindy was having a difficult time seeing the forest for the trees. ''If a feeling is negative and hurts, isn't it bad?''

''It may be undesirable, but it isn't bad. In fact, it is good.''

''Now I *am* confused. You're going to tell me that my bitterness is good. Get serious.''

''It's more than good. It's important, and you should be glad you have it.''

Cindy giggled. ''I think you ought to talk to a good shrink.''

I continued to point out something that is so obvious it is difficult to see. ''All your feelings are good, *simply because you are good and everything you feel is good also.* Your bitterness is important because you can learn from it. That scared little girl inside of you—I call her Wendy—is trying to tell you something. And if you call her 'bad' and try to banish her, she'll just keep hiding, but she won't go away. She is a part of you. Maybe you can help her grow up and not be afraid anymore. But you sure won't do it by calling her bad and trying to chase her away.''

''What you're telling me is that, in order to make these feelings go away, I have to quit trying to make them go away. That doesn't make any sense.''

"Let me say it this way. You want to move away from being a Wendy and become a Tinker, right?"

"Right."

"Well, how can you *move* if you don't start from somewhere?"

Her look was intense.

"You want me to help you stamp the badness out of you—the Wendy—and transform you into goodness—a Tinker. That will never work. And I wouldn't do it if I could."

I continued. "If I agree that I will help you get rid of so-called 'bad feelings,' then haven't I also agreed with your assessment of yourself as 'bad'?"

"You're telling me that, to change myself, I have to accept the way I am."

"Exactly! You are trapped by a dilemma. You want to stop mothering, but you don't want to stop caring. Rather than learn how to walk the thin line, you simply have given up trying. That is unfortunate and undesirable, but it's not bad. In fact, if you accept it, it is good. Once you accept it, you can begin to resolve the dilemma."

"That all sounds so simple."

"It is. In fact, it's so simple that it's tough to do. Imagine Wendy as a scared little girl. Reach out to her, help her, but don't damn her. She's not damnable. She is frightened and needs a friend. You can be her friend."

Cindy smiled. She felt the warmth of realizing that Wendy was a part of her, a good part of her. That realization pointed her to the way out of the trap. As long as she didn't damn Wendy, she could help her out of her trap.

Provided she didn't damn a part of herself, Cindy was ready to learn how to escape the mothering trap and resolve the Wendy Dilemma. In other words, she was ready to become a Tinker.

RESOLVING
THE WENDY
DILEMMA

PART IV

ESCAPE: BECOMING A TINKER

Becoming a Tinker is scary. It means confronting your Wendy responses and letting down the wall of defenses that protects you from the fear of rejection and feelings of inferiority. It means experimenting with your social image, controlling it because you *want* to, not because you have to. Most of all, it means confronting the Wendy Dilemma, changing the way you live, maybe the most frightening thing of all.

Change puts your hope to the test. As long as you keep your hope in your heart and away from reality, you always have it. But if you act out your hope and it proves futile, you've lost your ace in the hole. There is plenty of hope in the coming chapters. If one strategy fails, you'll find another and still another. One of them is bound to bring you some success and an increase in hope.

The following chapters summarize my work with women who were in one stage or another of becoming Tinkers. They wanted to accept responsibility for their own problems and make their lives better. They all had one thing in common: they wanted to resolve the Wendy Dilemma. As you read this section, don't look for the gold-edged map that has a giant X indicating treasure—total peace of mind. Such a map does not exist. If you expect to find it, you'll be sorely disappointed and end up bitter—not to mention mad at me.

When you look for an absolute answer outside yourself, you commit two errors: you give up control over your own destiny, and you imply that you don't have the right to be wrong. But you do! You have the right to be a Wendy. Once you've given yourself that right, you've begun to take control of your life and, eventually, your destiny. If you accept your Wendy responses without guilt or embarrassment, and add a little humor as you can, you'll find there is a natural force within that will drive you to find *your* answer. I can only help that process.

15

Learning to
Accept Wendy

"A part of me is troubled. Accepting it is more difficult than I ever would have believed."

There are two parts to Wendy's personality. First, there is a scared little girl. She is sweet, naive, and fearful. Second, there is a psuedo-mother. The psuedo-mother protects the scared little girl by being judgmental and possessive, and by doing her best to keep people away. She tries to shield the little girl from hurt. It is an alliance formed while Wendy was quite young.

The little girl wants to grow up and love a man; the mother knows the little girl may be rejected, so she keeps the man distant. One way the psuedo-mother ensures the little girl's safety is by finding a man who isn't grown up either. That becomes the man-child who will give Wendy a chance to love somebody while minimizing the risks of rejection.

All women have a bit of Wendy within the complicated, intrapsychic network called their personality. Wendy may have a minor role in a woman's life, surfacing only at rare moments; or a major one, dominating her daily behavior. Whatever the degree of presence, the first step in dealing with Wendy is learning to accept her.

Wendy has strengths and weaknesses. She has a fragile spirit and a tough exterior. If you try to banish her from your life, she will resist with all her might. Remember, she is an expert at dealing with rejection. In fact, she expects rejection. So when you reject the Wendy within you, she's ready for it. The psuedo-mother erects an immediate defense, attacking everything in her path in order to protect the little girl. Faced with her inability to protect herself, the little girl grows weaker and more insecure. When you reject the Wendy within you, you make her weaker, the psuedo-mother stronger, and both of them more resistant to change.

The secret of resolving the Wendy Dilemma is to accept the Wendy within you. (For men the secret of overcoming the Peter Pan Syndrome is to accept the scared little boy within them.) Accepting Wendy necessitates knowing who she is and how she relates to the rest of your personality. It's easy to see the Wendy in other women; it's tough to see her within yourself. But she can be found, heard, and understood. To do this, you must recognize a simple fact: personality is composed of many parts, and these parts communicate with each other through a system of internal speech. Not so surprisingly, we all talk to ourselves. When you find a way to eavesdrop on that conversation, you can unravel the mystery of how to help that scared little girl grow up.

Dr. Thomas Harris, in his book *I'm OK—You're OK,* popularized the idea of parts of ourselves communicating with each other. He identified three parts—parent, adult, and child—and called them "ego states." The parent tells the child what to do, the child tries to ignore the parent and do what feels the best, and the adult tries to monitor all forces so they won't self-destruct.

Faced with the excitement of a New Year's Eve party, the three parts might have the following conversation.

CHILD: "I want more booze, more food, more dancing, more . . ."

PARENT: "You've had enough of everything. Calm down, sober up, and go home."

CHILD: "I don't want to and you can't make me."

PARENT: "Oh, yes, I can."

CHILD: "Oh, no, you can't."

PARENT: "You just watch me, you insolent little devil."

ADULT: "All right, you two. Relax. Child, the parent is correct. If you eat and drink any more, you'll hurt yourself. Parent, understand that the child wants to have some fun. Ease off a bit."

It's the adult's job to monitor the child and the parent, balancing the forces of unbridled fun and strict morality. The adult is the voice of logic and information. In most people, the adult acts as the chairman of the board, helping all to express their viewpoints to the best of their ability. When things go as they are supposed to, the adult's logic and information decides what course of action will be followed.

I taught Cindy (Chapters 1 and 14) how to eavesdrop on her internal conversation. We began with the parent-adult-child triad and built from there. Once she was proficient, she was able to use her conscious adult to hear the scared little girl's plea for help, understand why Wendy projected a parental image, and help the mother to relax, the little girl to grow up.

The technique Cindy used is intended to externalize the internal conversation. It is called the gestalt psychodrama. It is "gestalt" because she was learning about the individual parts within her and working to put them together into a meaningful whole. It was "psychodrama" because she was giving an external presentation of neurological information through extended role-playing. She was acting out her inner conflicts.

Gestalt psychodrama was designed for use in group psychotherapy. However, with minor modifications, it can be employed in private by an individual who has a desire for self-knowledge and a flair for the dramatic. If you are unsuccessful with my version of gestalt psychodrama, you have two options. First, study Cindy's experience and see if anything in it applies to your life; or search out a group psychotherapist who will help you act out your dramatic investigation. The first option may be sufficient, since group psychotherapy research suggests that many people can profit from being "active observers."

Cindy participated in the psychodrama because she wanted to hear and understand her Wendy. If she had had serious psychological problems, I would have recommended individual psychotherapy as part of the psychodrama. But she was basically a well-adjusted person, so there was a good chance she could use the technique as a part of her ongoing process of self-discovery.

I recommended that she carry out her psychodrama in the privacy of a room that had at least four chairs. During our practice session in my office, I used three lounge chairs and a desk chair. We also found use for several plain pieces of paper and a pen.

Since Cindy had the capacity for spontaneity and I didn't want to bore her with prolonged explanations, she launched into her individual psychodrama, learning as she went.

"Let's begin by walking around the room; loosen up your muscles and get used to moving. In psychodrama, you have to put things into action."

I instructed her as we moved. "The first thing we have to do is warm up. It's best to start a psychodrama by getting the feel for what you're going to do. In this warm up, I'm going to ask you to do a little role-playing. Have you ever gotten a traffic ticket?"

She giggled. "Sure did. Going forty-two in a thirty-five-mile zone."

"Let's role-play that situation. Do you remember the first thing the policeman said to you?"

"Yes. 'Did you know you were speeding?' I said no, and then I started crying. I guess I was scared."

"Do you recall us talking about the parent-adult-child inside each person?"

"Yes."

"What part of you first answered the police-man—the parent, adult, or child?"

"I guess it would have to be the child. After all, I was scared and crying. That would be the child, right?"

"Right. Now, let's replay the scene and you role-play how the parent would respond. Remember, the parent judges, directs, and tells people what is right and wrong. Are you still with me?"

"Oh, yes, I know how the parent responds."

"Okay. Sit down in this chair. As you sit, I want you to be the parent responding to the officer."

When Cindy was seated, I set the scene. "I'm the officer and I've pulled you over. I'm about to walk up to you."

Remembering the state trooper who had last pulled me over, I did my best to imitate a serious-minded officer of the law. "Good-day, ma'am. May I see your license?"

I took the imaginary license from Cindy and said, "Do you know you were speeding?"

Cindy-as-parent answered, "You're wrong, sir, I wasn't speeding. After all, I would know if I was speeding. And I never speed. Your machine must be broken."

"You were going forty-two miles per hour in a thirty-five-mile-per-hour zone."

Cindy said, "Well, sir, I'm sorry to say this, but your nice little machine is wrong. I don't speed. I don't know how much clearer I can make it." Cindy was bristling.

I broke the scene. "Boy, you sure got into that role."

"Wow, I sure did. I was even angry at you."

"That simply means that you were successful in getting into the dramatic presentation of a real-life situation."

I moved across the room and gave her new instructions. "Now, let's try it again. Only this time, react as the adult would. Remember, the adult gives and asks for information, using logic as the guide. To give you the idea of change, I want you to sit in another chair."

She moved to another chair and said, "Fine."

I replayed my lines exactly as before. This time, Cindy had some trouble with the role, but played it fairly well.

"Officer, I'm not sure what you mean. I don't think I was speeding. May I see your radar?"

I complied.

"Is there any chance that your machine is wrong?"

"No, ma'am," I said.

"Well, that certainly is strange. I never speed. Are you certain I was in the thirty-five-mile-per-hour zone?"

I interrupted the scene and said, "That's fine. Do you have the idea of how to play different roles within the same situation?"

"Yes, I think so."

"Good. Now, let's move into a more complicated area. There are many personalities inside your head, not just parent, adult, and child. All of them represent a part of the real you. The first person I want you to pull out of your head is Wendy. I want you to put her in this chair. When you sit in this chair, you will be that part of Cindy who is a Wendy. But before you sit in the chair, I want you to think of the last time you remember Wendy coming out. Where were you, who was with you, and what were you doing?"

"Well, I'm not sure; I think Wendy came out last night. It was dinnertime and the kids were arguing over whose turn it was to set the table. I yelled at them to calm down and then I think I told Ed to help me. I don't know for sure what happened next. I remember the kids still fighting, and Ed stayed in the family room, reading his paper. Oh, I know, we got into this gigantic argument about the kids. That's right."

"I want you to look at last night as a movie. Try to remember a point in the movie where things really went sour. Recall, if you can, the one line that seemed to set you off."

Cindy recounted the scene out loud, detailing the words and action of the major players. As she moved slowly through the evening's events, she came across the critical line. I was asking Ed for his help with the kids and he said, 'You sure let those kids get away with murder.' That really set me off. I tried to stay calm and—"

"Hold it. Let's recreate the scene. Sit in your Wendy chair here and let's repeat what happened. I'll be Ed and you be yourself. You start by asking me for help and I'll say what Ed said. We'll see what happens."

I moved to the other side of the room, explaining that I was reading the paper in the family room. "All right. Sit down in the chair and I'll do my Ed imitation." I grabbed my notebook and held it out in front of me as though it were a newspaper. "Let's begin." I started humming as if I were thoroughly enjoying my reading.

Cindy said, "Ed, come help me with the kids."

I replied in a surly tone, "Damn, Cindy, you let those kids get away with murder."

Her eyebrows went up as her memory took her out of the therapy room and into her home. "I do not. They're good kids. They just have to be taught some manners."

Cindy had reacted defensively, so I pushed her. "I would teach them some manners, with the back of my hand."

"That's your answer for everything. If you had some feelings, you would know how that hurts." Cindy was whining.

"Feelings have nothing to do with it. You said you wanted some help with the kids and I told you how I'd help. But you won't let me." I had interjected a little-boy response from Ed.

Cindy moved into moderate martyrdom. "I try to be a good wife and mother, and I get no help from you. I end up having to take care of *your* children all by myself." The sarcastic emphasis upon *your* signaled the beginning of mild punishment.

Even though I was playing a role, I felt dumbfounded. I had received a small slap on the hands. I stuck with what I thought Ed might say. "You like to pick on me after I've had a hard day, don't you?" Ed would likely use a guilt trip as a passive-aggressive maneuver intended to get Cindy off his back.

This last comment had its effect. Cindy lost her concentration and said, "Gosh, the same old stuff! It always ends up the same way."

I slipped back into the here-and-now also. "Did we role-play that scene accurately?"

"You better believe it! Too accurately. I could have come over there and hit you."

"Okay. Give that a voice."

"What?"

"Let's continue pulling parts of Cindy out of your head. I just heard another part. Anger. Move into another chair and give anger its say. Go ahead. When you sit in that chair, you are the part of Cindy that is angry. Sit down and *be* angry."

Cindy moved into a chair a few feet away and sat motionless for a moment. "I don't know what to say."

"Just say how you feel." I pushed her a little. "You were ready to clobber Ed over there. Well, give it to him, only do it with words."

"I really don't like you talking to me that way." Her statement was stilted and dry, as if she had read it from a textbook.

"You're having a tough time being angry, aren't you?"

"When I sit here, I can't feel it."

"But you could feel it over here, when you were being Wendy."

"Yes."

"Well, come back over here and try it again."

Cindy moved back to her Wendy chair, sat down, and with very little prompting, started badgering Ed. "You're a little boy, a scared little boy. You haven't got the guts to get involved with a woman, a real woman. You feel sorry for yourself, you run around acting like a big shot, but the people who should come first—your family—you just ignore. And you expect me to do everything *you* want, but you won't do what I want."

She paused, so I jumped in. "How does that feel?"

"Good and bad. Good because that's the way I feel. Bad because . . . I don't know, just something feels bad."

Cindy hit a temporary block, a signal that we should move around the room and take a fresh look at what had occurred.

"Let's walk around the room and talk about what we have here. When you were Wendy, you went through several reactions. First, you apologized for the kids, then you started whining, then you moved into some self-pity and a zinger about *his* kids."

"Yuck! That stinks. What a jerk."

I broke off my analysis and looked at Cindy in silence, punctuating my comment before I said it. "Who keeps calling you nasty names?"

"I don't know."

I seized the moment, pointed to another chair, and said, "Sit in this chair and repeat what you just said about being a jerk."

Cindy sat down without breaking her concentration. "It's true. When I . . . I mean, when Cindy behaves that way, she *is* a jerk and it *does* stink. She's letting that man make her talk in goofy ways. He's running her into the ground and she doesn't do anything about it except whine and try to get even. She really ought to grow up."

I gently grabbed Cindy by the shoulder, walked with her to the other side of the room, and, in a conspiratorial tone, reached out to her voice of adult logic by saying, "Well, Dr. Cindy, as a newly appointed junior shrink, what is your opinion about what this lady is saying?"

Cindy enjoyed the role switch. "I would say she has a terrible case of lousy self-esteem. She is much too hard on herself."

I continued my consultation. "Maybe someone should tell her that; someone she'd trust. There must be somebody else inside this patient's head who can talk to her so that she'll listen."

Moving away from the scene helped Cindy gain added perspective. "There is. There's another side to her that isn't very strong. But it's there."

"Let's go see if we can get it out." Cindy and I moved back to the growing circle of chairs, and I pointed to the one in which anger had had a difficult time speaking. "Last time we tried to put anger in this chair, it didn't work. Let's try to put something more positive in it. Sit down in the chair and talk to Wendy"—I pointed to the Wendy chair—"about what you think of her behavior."

"Wendy, you really have to shape up. You know that." Cindy had a smile in her voice. "You're a nice kid, you really are. But you let yourself get involved in all sorts of stupid things. Don't argue with Ed. He's just being a child. When you argue with him, you're being a child, too."

It was time for Cindy to learn how to carry out the refined points of the psychodrama—have parts of herself carry on dialogue with one another. I stood next to Cindy and motioned with my hand. "Move into Wendy's chair and answer the voice we just heard."

Cindy moved, collected her thoughts, and said, "How am I supposed to make him change? I don't want to lose him. But I don't want him the way he is. Do you have an answer for that one?"

Cindy's concentration was momentarily broken. But she got it back, proving she was getting accustomed to the drama. "I want to call Wendy stupid for saying these things. I guess I should be in that chair." She pointed to the one where the voice of self-damning had come from.

She needed only minimal direction. "Do it."

Cindy moved into the damning chair and said, "You sound so childish." Now there was a snarl in Cindy's voice. "Why can't you grow up and see the world for what it is. Quit being such a baby."

With a sudden burst of insight, Cindy interrupted herself and said, "That's my mother. That's my mother talking. Do you realize that? This is my mother sitting here. She doesn't like Wendy at all. She thinks she's foolish for wanting more than she's got."

I kept pushing. "Well, is there anybody who can talk back to her?"

"Wendy sure can't. But this chair can." Cindy got up and sat down in the yet-unnamed chair. She turned to the mother chair and said, "Leave the girl alone. You've been telling her what to think long enough. She has to live her own life and she can't live it the way you do."

The pause signaled the end of an interaction. I motioned Cindy to join me in the consultation corner. I didn't have to push her to use her adult to analyze the situation.

"There's the parent, adult, and child over there. Wendy is the child, mother is the parent, and the other chair is the adult."

"It's a little more complicated than that. Wendy is a scared little girl, but she also has a caustic parental part who martyrs herself and punishes others. The mother is bitter with her own life and she's dumping on Wendy. And the other chair really isn't pure adult, because she has the strong opinions in certain directions."

Cindy was moving quickly. "The mother is really a Wendy too, isn't she?"

Her role-playing gave way to added insight. "My mother is just a sad, scared little girl who never grew up, isn't she? That's exactly how I'll be with my daughter, isn't it?''

I reassured her. "Not if you keep working and growing the way you are right now."

"But how do I do that? I can't keep going to therapy the rest of my life."

"Of course not. Are you saying that there's nothing inside of you that can help you?"

"I guess that one chair could help. But I don't know what that is."

"Let me give you a hint or two. It's a voice of self-confidence, of a person who isn't afraid to say what's on her mind. She knows how to laugh, have a good time, and not get trapped by other people's childishness. She exists inside your head, but she's not very strong. That's because she usually gets drowned out by Wendy and her mother." I decided to make her guess.

"She sounds great to me. I just wish I knew who she was."

"Well, imagine that your Ed comes up to this woman and says, 'You let your kids get away with murder.' Can you hear her say, 'You silly ass'?"

The lights went on in Cindy's head. There was a twinkle in her eye and a smile on her face. She said, "That's Tinker, isn't it? Yeah, that's Tinker all right."

I nodded my head.

In an expression of spontaneity, Cindy walked over to the Tinker chair, sat down, and triumphantly exclaimed, "I'm staying here forever."

"Wanna bet?" I said.

"Sure. I'll just get rid of those chairs. I'll put them out in your waiting room." She was half serious.

"You and I both know it won't work that way. Wendy is a big part of you. You can't just banish her. You have to help her."

"Grow up, right?"

"Right. And not be afraid. And learn how to say nice things about herself rather than tearing herself down all the time."

"What do I do about mother over here?"

"Yeah, what *do* you do?"

"I guess she has to grow up, too. But if that doesn't work, I don't know."

"There will be many things to learn. But if you trust yourself, you'll figure it out." I reminded her of one of her own statements. " 'It really will work out.' Provided you work at it."

"How do I work at it?"

"Just as you've done today. Getting all the parts of yourself out in the open and letting them talk to one another."

"But Wendy is such a wimp."

I gave her a did-you-hear-yourself look and she recanted.

"I know, I know; I shouldn't cut her down. I didn't mean that the way my mother would say it. I meant it like, she's okay, but she's a wimp." Cindy was laughing.

"One serious point, Cindy. You'll never help Wendy grow up if you cut her down, make fun of her, or try to throw her out of your life. That's what

I meant when I said, 'Don't damn Wendy.' If you think back over our session today, you'll recall that there are a lot of harsh words going on in your life. A lot of damning. If you damn Wendy, you are actually damning yourself. Wendy will hide behind that mother façade and you'll never be able to help her deal with her fears. But if you accept her for what she is, you have a chance to help her.

"If Wendy remains a scared little girl, her fears will be stronger than Tinker's voice. Tinker will remain in the background, and I don't think you want that to happen."

"Absolutely not. But I'm not sure what Tinker wants to do. Maybe she's not grown up either."

"That may be true, but she sure will learn fast. If Wendy learns to accept herself, she will grow up and give way to Tinker. And Tinker will find the way."

"Where do I start?"

"Right where you are."

16

Resolving Your Dependency Needs

"It was extremely hard to admit that my mother often used me to escape her own pain, and that my father didn't know how to say 'I love you.' Now that I accept that, I've forgiven them. It's easier to live with myself."

Once a woman has accepted her Wendy (even though she may still smile and call her "a silly ass"), her next step is to resolve her dependency needs. As you'll recall from Chapter 3, these are the needs of comfort, security, and belonging, things a child expects from his or her parents. When these needs are not met, the child may experience a fear of abandonment. (In an adult, this fear typically becomes one of rejection.)

As a little girl, a Wendy may have coped with this fear by trying to be the perfect daughter to her mother. This may have included helping to mother her father. That's when her Wendy began.

A woman who coped with her fear of abandonment by mothering the first man she loved has been living, to one degree or another, in a state of bondage toward all men ever since. If this applies to you,

you probably have a biased view of the men in your life. Whenever you begin to care about a man, you experience a flashback to the fear of abandonment that causes you to run away from adult love and hide in the sanctuary of mothering. No matter what the grown-up inside of you wants, the fearful little girl will force you to do whatever is necessary to avoid the possibility of rejection.

If you wish to become a Tinker and enjoy the freedom of loving, you will have to confront your fear of rejection. You will have to take a trip back into your childhood, not to dig up useless old memories, but to put the past behind you, once and for all. The Wendy inside you must let go of the past in order to give your Tinker a chance to live in the present. Yet letting go of the past is easier said than done. There are many obstacles to overcome.

As you struggle to resolve the past, the biggest of these obstacles is the feeling of having wasted so much time. Events, times, places, and dates run through your mind. You don't want to live your entire life over, just a few critical situations. You could have made a different decision, eliminating much of the turmoil you now are forced to live with. One woman had a difficult time coping with "wasted years."

"The hardest part is to realize that I didn't learn from my mistakes. I kept doing the same thing time after time, man after man. You know, I think I could have made my first marriage work, if only I had known what I know now. And the kids wouldn't have had to live through the pain they did.

That wasn't fair to them—to bring them into a family where neither parent was grown up.''

If you share any part of this woman's regret, you'll want to adjust your attitude so that remorse and penitence don't become a way of life. You'll need to learn a fundamental skill: how to feel sad. Be careful before you dismiss this suggestion as simplistic. It's more critical than you might think.

Most people don't give themselves the right to experience unencumbered sadness. By unencumbered, I mean experiencing sadness without adding pity, denial, revenge, and other emotions intended to dull the pain. Realizing that past mistakes have been repeated *needlessly* hurts. Allow room in the circle of mental chairs for sadness. When you sit in that chair, cry and feel bad. That's all there is to do. If you don't give sadness a place of its own, you are bound to repeat the mistakes again, and waste even more time.

Once you know how to feel sad, old wounds will start to heal and you will give less time to feeling sad. You'll have more energy for other activities aimed at resolving dependency needs. That's when another major obstacle may seem to pop out of nowhere and threaten to consume you—anger.

When the Wendy in you begins to grow up, she will unleash negative feelings that may have been repressed for decades. Seemingly unrelated temper tantrums may fill your head. The voices of anger may overlap and drown one another out. Individually, they might sound something like this:

"I hate you, Mom. You let Dad run you into the

ground. You were a slave to him. Just when I needed you to show me how to be a grown-up, you acted like a scared little servant girl. And you taught me to do the very same thing.

"Damn you, Dad. You were so self-centered you couldn't reach out and hug me. You always came first. You made me feel as if something was wrong with me, and all the time it was you. You weren't man enough to love your wife and children with your heart. You tried to do it with your pocketbook. Worst of all, you never said you loved me. I hate you for that most of all."

The anger is more understandable if you recognize it as the voice of a little girl fighting the fear of abandonment and trying to regain a sense of self-worth. (Remember, anger is usually seen as the flip side of fear.) Anger, too, should have a place in your gestalt. If you give it a voice and clarify it, anger can actually be an indispensable help in the resolution of your dependency needs. Unless you legitimize your anger and see it in the proper perspective, you may never resolve the Wendy Dilemma.

Anger can point you in the direction of change. But you must do more than simply vent it whenever you feel it. When you give anger a voice, write it down on a piece of paper and move to your Tinker chair, leaving the paper on the anger chair. Then, from your Tinker position, respond to the anger with suggestions for changing the situation.

I've helped countless women vent their anger. However, after their catharsis I always challenge them: ''What are you going to do about it?'' From here there are usually two general options, both dependent upon whether or not the woman's parents are still living. Before discussing strategies for these two options, we must first talk about the general technique to be employed whatever the circumstances: self-assertion.

Self-assertion is verbal behavior exhibited for the purpose of declaring one's thoughts or feelings so that they can be understood and/or acted upon by another person. A recent study evaluated five major self-assertion rating scales and, through a statistical technique called factor analysis, reduced hundreds of self-assertive behaviors down to the lowest possible number. The study concluded that almost half of all self-assertions fall into two broad categories: first, the ability to stand up for one's rights in public places; and second, initiating contact with a nonintimate person. Since a woman who wants to resolve fear and anger toward her parents is not on an intimate basis with them, but wishes to initiate contact on a new subject, her self-assertion would fall into the second category.

Further research on self-assertion suggests that when a person first initiates contact in an unfamiliar area, she is taking a risk. Risks involve anxiety, and the best way to reduce anxiety is to move one step at a time, tackling easier problems before advancing to more difficult ones.

The upshot of this introductory information is that, as you aim to resolve your dependency needs, you may reduce your risk and anxiety if you first assert yourself in a situation with fewer emotional overtones than with your parents. Hence, you may wish to warm up for a confrontation with your parents by practicing assertion in the first of the two categories mentioned above. In short, confront a salesperson or store clerk before taking on your mother or father. You'll find warm-up suggestions in Chapter 18, "Practicing the Tinker Response."

However you work your way up to it, confronting your parents will be scary. If the one you would have wished to confront is deceased, you will have to use the psychodrama technique. For this, you'll need the help of a friend or counselor; confronting an emotional memory is too complicated to be executed without assistance.

Say, for example, you wish to confront your deceased father about his lack of warmth.

First, write down a few of the things that you remember him saying. Project the kinds of things he might have said about you by consulting your mother or another living relative who knew your father well. Write these down also. Put these things in a chair opposite you. If you have a friend who can help, explain what you want him or her to do; that is, play the part of your father by reading the items on the paper. Talking to your friend about your father may help him or her role-play the part more realistically. If you use a counselor, make sure he or she understands the elements of psychodrama.

Next, state your major concern, question, or complaint in clear, unequivocal language. Write it down if that will help. Say it out loud several times before role-playing. Use this procedure as a warm-up.

Start the role-playing by stating your concern. The other party should use the script you prepared as a guide in responding, feeling free to ad lib within the boundaries set by the script.

This is how a typical psychodramatic conversation might sound:

YOU: "I want to know why you didn't tell me that you loved me."

FRIEND-AS-FATHER: "You knew I always loved you."

YOU: "But why didn't you show it or tell me?"

F-A-F: "I thought you knew. I told your mother how much you meant to me."

YOU: "But you didn't tell me. That really hurt a lot."

F-A-F: "I had a lot of things on my mind. You really shouldn't complain. You had everything you ever wanted."

YOU: "Except a father."

Don't force the conversation. It isn't necessary that some earth-shaking resolution be reached. It's sufficient that you have a chance to state your concerns within the restrictive limits available in the psychodramatic procedure. Remember, the ultimate resolution will occur *inside* your head, whether your parents are alive or not. That is the crucially important lesson to be learned from this exercise.

If the parent to be confronted is alive, the encounter holds much more promise—and anxiety. A personal confrontation will bring you face-to-face with your fear of rejection and your feelings of inferiority. You will want to run away or find last-minute excuses to avoid the scene.

You can prepare for the confrontation and desensitize some of your fear by acting out a psychodrama in advance. Follow the same procedure used if the parent is deceased. You don't necessarily need a confidant to help you with the practice session. Your written script is all the help you'll need.

Finding the right time and place for the confrontation is another challenge. Beyond insuring privacy, there is no perfect time. Except for one woman who tried to do it over the telephone (and failed), all the women I've dealt with have carried out the confrontation in a one-on-one situation.

Here are some examples of how women have confronted their parents concerning unresolved dependency needs.

After Thanksgiving dinner while they were both alone in the kitchen, Diane, realizing that her mother was relaxed and approachable, said, "Mom, I always had the feeling that I was in the way of you and Dad."

Mom seemed shocked and replied, "How could you think such a thing?"

Diane didn't pay much attention to what her mother said. She was nervous, so she just kept talking. "When I had a problem, you seemed to dismiss it. Once a bully scared me real bad after school. When I told you, you said, 'Don't be a baby. Stand up for yourself.' But I didn't know how. I wanted you to tell me that he was bad. But you made it seem like I'd done something wrong. I wanted to tell Dad, but I heard you tell him and you both laughed about it. That hurt me real bad.''

Diane's mother responded as Diane had predicted. She heaped blame on herself, lamenting how she had always tried to do her best, but that must not have been good enough. At first, Diane felt guilty for bringing up the subject. But the next day she realized that her mother always used the martyr routine to blunt criticism; that was just the way she was. Although her confrontation didn't change her mother, it did give Diane a boost in self-confidence. In confronting her mother, she had confronted her own insecurity and found out that it wasn't her problem. Her mother was more insecure than Diane had ever been.

Victoria was going to take her father to lunch at his favorite restaurant until I suggested that she go to a place where *she* felt most comfortable. She did. She warmed herself up to the confrontation by talking about one of her father's favorite subjects—his granddaughter. She thanked him for paying so much attention to the little girl, and then added, ''You know, I sometimes get jealous of the way you hug Cindy and hold her on your lap. I would have given anything if you'd done that with me.'' She had planned on stopping at this point and she did.

Her father became flustered. He turned red and stammered as he tried to talk. ''I did hold you when you were a little girl. You sat on my lap almost every night.''

Her father's apologetic tone encouraged Victoria.

"But you quit. All of a sudden, you just quit. You treated me as if I had a disease. That hurt so bad. I never understood why."

He did his best to explain. "Well, you started to become a young lady. And, well, I thought it was time that you grew up. You weren't daddy's little girl anymore. You know . . . you were growing up."

Victoria felt angry. "So, *you* decided that I didn't need your love anymore. That's a dirty thing to do to a little girl."

"But you weren't little anymore."

"I thought I was. Didn't you ever think of me and what I needed?"

"Vicky, when a little girl starts to fill out, it's time for a father to back off. She has to become a young lady and find herself a man."

It took twenty-seven years, but the light finally went on in Victoria's head. She remained quiet as she thought to herself, "I was filling out—sure. My puberty came early. He saw my body develop and he backed off. He got scared!"

Victoria thought about the confrontation for days. It was hard for her to realize that her father had had a sexual stirring within him when he saw his daughter becoming a woman. The feeling had scared him. The thought embarrassed Victoria. But the more she thought about it, the more empathy she gained for her father. He was not good at understanding his feelings, and his old-world, traditional upbringing had gotten the best of him. He had run away from a natural reaction, probably thinking of himself as some kind of pervert. In the anxiety that followed, he never thought of what it did to his daughter. He never considered talking about it with his wife and figuring out the best way to explain his feelings. If he could have accepted his reaction, he would have overcome it and continued to hug his daughter. Realizing the panic and turmoil her father had gone through gave Victoria an entirely new outlook on old feelings.

Peg was a brave soul. She decided to confront both her parents at the same time. According to her evaluation, some of the heat would be taken off her because her parents would be careful of what they said in front of each other.

Every time she considered a subtle way of initiating the conversation, she ended up getting confused. So, after writing down what she wanted to say, she invited herself to their house, sat them down in the living room, and simply began to read her little speech.

"I have felt inferior all my life and I think most of it is your fault. Both of you put me in the middle and used me so you wouldn't have to deal with your problems. Mom, you always told me that Dad couldn't express his feelings, but that he wanted me to know that he loved me. Why in hell did you let him off the hook like that?

"Dad, you always made excuses for me when I acted like a bitch toward Mom. You slipped me money when Mom said I couldn't have any. You bought me things that Mom said I shouldn't have. You let me get away with murder, and then you'd turn around and make a big fuss over me when your friends were around, calling me 'your special little princess.' I wasn't special to you; I was a little *thing* you had to show off when you wanted to look good.''

By the time she was finished, Peg was practically screaming. Her hands were sweating, her breathing was shallow, and she was drunk with power, fear, and guilt, all rolled into one. Nothing they could say could make things worse for her. But she certainly wasn't ready for what she heard.

Her father, of all people, spoke firmly. ''You're probably right in everything you've said. Your mother and I have talked of getting a divorce. But after this many years, we just don't want to start over again. We've begun marriage counseling to see if we can't work something out. We were going to tell you whenever we got up the nerve. All we can say now is that we are sorry.'' Her mother nodded in agreement.

Peg started giggling. It was terribly inappropriate, but her anxiety suddenly turned into hysteria. Her father's words rang inside her head. *''Whenever we got up the nerve.''* Peg couldn't believe her parents were so scared. She started crying. The walls of misunderstanding crumbled; she ran across the room and hugged them both, apologizing for her burning indictment. Three human beings, with tears streaming down their faces, clutched one another as if touching were essential to their survival.

Each woman's experience provides an additional lesson. Diane learned she could gain a new perspective on her life without her mother truly hearing any part of a confrontation. Peg could have saved herself a great deal of turmoil if she had confronted her parents earlier. Her story suggests that your parents might be feeling just as bad as (or worse than) you are.

Victoria's story demonstrates an exception to the general rule; that is, her fear of rejection developed later in her life, at or near puberty. Her father misinterpreted his sexual reaction to his daughter. Rather than resolve it through confidential conversations, he elected to push Victoria away, justifying it with his old-fashioned chauvinistic ideas. Victoria viewed this as a rejection that somehow had something to do with her getting older. Since the rejection occurred *after* she had experienced some warmth and affection from her father, Victoria's Wendy was more mature than most. Her voice of inferiority was weaker than usual, giving her a better chance of escaping the trap.

Reflecting on eighteen years of clinical experience gave me another insight into the resolution process. That is, most women feel compelled to confront their mothers about a variety of issues: child rearing, sex, guilt, and high expectations, to name a few. Poor mom seems to take the most heat when it comes time to resolve dependency needs. But what about dad? Did he not have an impact on your upbringing? The fact that he was in the background doesn't release him from his responsibility. In fact, it could be that his refusal or inability to join in partnership with your mother in raising you contributed more to your unresolved dependency needs than anything your mother did or did not do. Therefore, if you consider confronting your parents in an attempt to put the past to rest, keep in mind that the encounter between you and your father may be more important (and more difficult) than that with your mother.

Diane, Peg, and Victoria each found a special meaning from her confrontation. Obviously not all confrontations will have a positive resolution. More often than not, the best that happens is the woman overcomes her fear of rejection and feeling of inferiority enough to believe that she has the right to confront her parents. That's why many women dig up old memories, practice the words of confrontation, designate a time and place for the encounter, and then feel so good about having had the courage to consider the confrontation that they don't have to actually do it.

There are ways of controlling the influence of unresolved dependency needs without involving an all-out confrontation. If your parents are deceased and you find no relief in the psychodrama technique, or they are alive and you just don't want to confront them, here are suggestions for conscious avoidance of Wendy responses.

DIARY OF MOTHERING SCRIPTS

If you know that a confrontation would only cause more bad feelings between you and your parents, consider keeping a diary of mothering scripts. Each time you talk with your parents, either in person or by phone, take notes after the conversation. Listen carefully to the things your mother says to you and to your father that represent a Wendy response. Write down examples of denial, overprotection, possessiveness, complaining, judgmentalism, martyrdom, and punishment. Review these diaries from time to time, looking for verbalizations that may have creeped into your relationships with other adults. This method helps you identify your Wendy responses by reviewing the present-day communication between you and the person who may have taught you how to mother your man.

REALIGN PARENTING SKILLS

Use the same general technique to evaluate your parenting skills with your children (if applicable). Ask yourself these questions: Do I use guilt in trying to discipline my kids? ("How could you hurt me this way?") Do I complain continuously with no other follow-through? Do I overlook punishable behavior, saying such things as, "Well, that's just how kids are these days"? Am I excessive in protecting or judging my children?

Affirmative answers to the above suggest that your inappropriate mothering script has spilled over into areas in which your mothering skills are truly important. Using rational disciplinary techniques can remind you to separate mothering your children from mothering your man.

EXTINCTION

Martha, an enterprising young woman, wanted nothing to do with confrontation or diaries. She believed she could eventually overcome her dependency needs if her mother would just stop treating her like a little girl. Not only was the past not dead, but it was also recreated several times a week.

Therefore, the woman set out on a simple but effective program we'll call "extinction." She actively ignored her mother every time her mother behaved in an overprotective, excessively judgmental, or self-sacrificial manner. When her mother said, "Now, dear, remember to tell Mack (her husband) that you want to go to dinner on your birthday," Martha went beyond simply ignoring by responding, "You know, Mom, I'd like a new blouse for my birthday. Could you get me one?" This abrupt change in the subject, complete with a leading question, tended to "extinguish" the mother's good-natured meddlesomeness. When Martha responded similarly to other instances of inappropriate mothering, her mother eventually got the idea and eliminated much of her offensive behavior.

As the Wendy woman puts the past into inactive memory, she may find herself confronting other mother figures in her life. A female supervisor, the chairwoman of a social group, and the leader of a charity organization may provide a renewed challenge for a Tinker-in-training. One woman found she was unable to accept responsibility for her own life until she confronted her mother-in-law.

"I had resolved my hang-up with my mom and dad only to be faced with my mother-in-law. I had transferred many insecure feelings to her. I permitted her to interfere in my life because I was afraid of her disapproval. Once I realized what I was doing, I was able to stop it. I might add, it was much easier with her than with my mother. I just hung up on her.

"It all started when my best friend told me that my mother-in-law had been asking her about my marital problems. Well, I called 'Mother dear' and told her that my marital situation was between me and my husband and that I didn't appreciate her talking to my best friend about it.

"She, of course, didn't listen to me, and just started lecturing me about how to take care of her son. So, with a calm voice, I interrupted her and told her, as nicely as possible, that if she didn't listen to me, I was going to hang up on her. She didn't pay any attention to me. She just kept lecturing. So I hung up immediately. I knew I was right.

"By the way, the next time we talked, she was gracious, if not a little distant. The kids even said, 'Mom, something's wrong with Grandma; she was nice today.' "

There are many paths to resolving your needs for love, belonging, and comfort from your parents. And, as this last case illustrates, just about the time you think you have it all under control, your inferiority has a way of popping up somewhere else. It's safe to say that, after being suppressed for many years, Wendy does not grow up overnight.

Wendy will not let go of the past until she concludes her search. With the icons of maturity all about you, it's a challenge to remember that Wendy is just a scared little girl wandering around inside your mind, searching for something she lost.

If you sit your Wendy in a chair and ask her what she's looking for, she'll probably speak in riddles. "I don't know. Something. Not an expensive something, but something that is very important to me. Like my teddy bear—I called it 'foo-foo,' or my Raggedy Ann doll, I called her 'foo-foo' too. But neither one of those is it. I don't know what it is, call it my 'foo-foo,' but it exists and I lost it."

Those of you who share this search try to banish Wendy from your life. You do your best to deny the existence of her childish search or to repress her desire. If and when you go back home (wherever that may be), you put Wendy in a back room of your mind, tell her to stay quiet, and then interact with the other adults in "grown-up" conversations. You talk to your parents about marriage, children, careers, and friends. You're careful to avoid emotion-laden subjects. If one comes up, it is uncomfortable. As you walk away from the encounter, you can hear Wendy's steady whisper: "Please let me out. I want to search for my missing foo-foo."

If Wendy is to grow up, you must help her hunt for her foo-foo. Maybe she needs to realize that it wasn't her fault that her father didn't hug her; maybe she needs to find that she isn't bound by her mother's definition of womanhood; maybe she needs to find a way to communicate with the memory of a departed parent; maybe she needs to discover new ways of reacting to her parents' same old ways of doing things; maybe it's something even deeper.

You'll never find out what your Wendy needs until you help her take a trip back in time. Use all your mental resources to help her in this journey. It will be an adventure, much like Wendy's flight into Never-Never Land. But unlike Wendy, you will recognize that you are on a special mission. You will return when you find what you're searching for. One woman found the meaning she was hunting for, but once she found it, she realized she didn't need it.

"I was obsessed with anger and disappointment toward my mother. Once I confronted her, I could feel nothing but pity for her. She is a very sad lady, who never knew what it was like to be truly loved.

"I always felt sorry for my father. Once I confronted him, I realized that he was a very weak man. I would have given anything if only he had hugged me and told me he loved me. When I finally realized that he'll never be able to do that, I must have cried for two days."

This woman had spent thirty years of her life waiting for her father to tell her he loved her. Such a simple thing. She remembers hearing it from her mother, but that wasn't enough. She wanted it from Dad. She never got it. When she accepted the fact that it wasn't her fault that she had never heard it, she was free. Once free, she didn't need to hear it anymore, not from him anyway.

This woman wanted to hear "I love you" from the man in her life; not from a father figure, but from a grown-up man. She didn't know whether he was capable of saying it *and* showing her that he meant it, but she was bound and determined to find out. She finally silenced the voice of inferiority and realized she *deserved* to hear "I love you." She wasn't going to mother him anymore, pretending that if she pleased him he would fill her father's shoes. This woman threw away her childhood security blanket and went looking for love and belonging in the real world. This was her only chance to stop living in the past and find a grown-up foo-foo. Because she loved herself, she had no doubt that she would find it.

17

Loving, Not Mothering

"I want to stop being his mother and start being his wife. I have a lot of good years left and I want to spend them with the man I love."

After twenty-five years, this woman still has the hope that more love will come into her life. Although she regrets being trapped in the Wendy Dilemma, she's not ashamed to admit it.

"Sure I mothered him. It was the biggest mistake of my life. The first time he came to me—twenty-five years ago—and started whining about his mother, I should have kicked him in the pants and told him to grow up and either pick me or his mother. *And* stuck to my guns."

The spark of energy that promises a new day and a new way of loving is evident in this woman's gentle self-chiding. So is her sense of humor. She's not taking herself too seriously. She's very wise. A positive attitude is critical in overcoming the Wendy responses and becoming a Tinker. Laughter helps you relax, breathe a little deeper, regain your rational senses a little quicker, and consider a fresh alternative to an old problem.

As you move toward change and alternatives for

action, keep in mind lessons learned by other women.

"I almost forced myself to think only of the horrible things he had done to me. It made me feel less guilty when I thought about leaving him. But it wasn't fair. He wasn't always a cruel man. In fact, there were, and still are, times when he can be kind and gentle. That makes my anger even more confusing. Let's face it, I wouldn't still be with him if I hadn't played along with his moods. I'm partially to blame."

Another woman confided that she would have had an easy time deciding what to do about her relationship if her man had been assaultive. But the fact that he had a boyish quality and a sulky manner made her feel terrible when she thought of divorce.

You don't become a Tinker in a vacuum. There are many people in your life, many of whom may stimulate the fear of rejection, pleasing-through-mothering cycle. This chapter focuses on your relationship with a man, even if you see him only occasionally. As you stop mothering and start loving, you may be accused of being self-centered or of simply using a man as an emotional guinea pig. Here's how a young woman working to become a Tinker responded to this criticism.

"Sure I'm self-centered. I'm going to start doing the best things I can for myself, and that includes *not* being anybody's mother. I have some things to learn about being a whole person, and it may take some time and some different experiences. And that may mean different guys. As for using them, yeah, if you're a dyed-in-the-wool pessimist, you could look at it that way. I prefer to think that I'm using myself to grow up, just as the guy should be doing.

"The other night I met this neat guy and we had dinner and then decided to go back to my place. He turned me on and I wanted him. He was a nice guy and I decided I could trust him. So I was honest. I told him I was using that night's experience to see how I felt being the sexual aggressor. We had great sex and then we talked about how men and women become afraid to be honest. I'm seeing him again this weekend."

Since learning to love is a lifelong process, you should be ready for many lively experiences as you leave the Wendy trap. Each of you has that spark of Tinker energy somewhere inside. You can use it to get past your fears, take some risks, and move away from a life of boring repetitiousness and stagnation.

THE ADULT LOVE SCRIPT

If the above messages rekindle hope inside and make you want to learn how to love, not mother, you'll need a place to begin. That place is with the adult love script. Unlike the script for the mothering role, the adult love script, if used correctly, can teach you to throw away all psychological scripts. It's a script that teaches you to develop your own lines rather than memorize somebody else's words or thoughts.

When you love someone, there isn't a script to tell you how to express that love. Sure we have expectations of how we want our love life to go. But if we are truly in love, there should be no need to demand that the partner meet narrowly defined expectations. Learning how to love in an adult way is learning to let go of expectations, rules, demands, and imperatives. We learn to take what we get the way it is given.

There are, however, certain attributes that, in an objective sense, make for a productive love relationship. These attributes comprise the adult love script. It is this script that will help you stop mothering and start loving your man. Here is a brief outline of the components of the adult love script.

Give-and-take	Lovers know how to make compromises without pity or regret, and occasionally make concessions with a strong belief that the other partner will reciprocate in kind.
Tolerance and empathy	Lovers will endure inconvenience and even hurt because they have empathy for their partner.
Dependability	Lovers depend upon each other. They know that if all else fails, the loved one will be there to do whatever he or she can to help.
Personal development	Lovers never forget that they are individuals with differing needs. Each is free to pursue personal development in areas of career, education, hobbies, and friends.

Sharing	Lovers freely share their thoughts, opinions, feelings, and perspectives on life. There is no judging of people, only facts.
Realism	Lovers accept that occasionally their love life won't go well. They do not attempt to resolve *every* conflict or disagreement. Some minor conflicts can be ignored once it is clear that continued discussion will lead nowhere.
Intimacy	Lovers touch, hug, kiss, hold hands, and freely express erotic pleasures with one another. Within their intimacy is plenty of room for playfulness.
The X factor	Lovers recognize that there is an unspoken bond between them. It is a special feeling of closeness and is unnamed and undefinable; hence the label the X factor.

The adult love script helps you learn how to accept responsibility *only* for your strengths and weaknesses. With it you can learn to stop taking responsibility for your man's problems and start working on your own. As you practice following the adult love script, you stop saying things like, "What can I do to make him change?" The adult love script answers, "Nothing."

The adult love script promotes a resolution of the Peter Pan Syndrome and the Wendy Dilemma.

Through it, you can learn to love in a grown-up way. The adult love script teaches you to merge the skills in your head with the feelings in your heart. It introduces you to a new era of loving, in which you are free to express your vulnerability without running away from your fears.

Warning: If you employ the adult love script on your way to becoming a Tinker, you will, by definition, *not* try to make your man change. Be forewarned: adult love is conditional. Therefore, if he doesn't sooner or later start expressing his love to you in a way that is compatible with your personality and wishes, or if he refuses to participate with you in learning the adult love script, there is every reason to believe that you will eventually leave him.

In the rest of this chapter you will learn how to implement the adult love script with the man in your life and, in so doing, resolve the Wendy Dilemma. That means you'll have to replace your Wendy responses with traits of adult love. For the sake of clarity, I have matched up attributes of adult love with Wendy responses, suggesting that a specific love trait can have a special impact on a Wendy response. Therefore, if you are concerned about your denial, you'll find the most help in the section that explains how to add realism to your relationship. If judgment is a weakness, you should improve the sharing of your opinions and feelings.

Wendy Response	Adult Love Trait
Martyrdom	Give-and-take
Punishment	Tolerance and empathy

Overprotection	Dependability
Possessiveness	Personal development
Judgment	Sharing
Denial	Realism
Complaining	Intimacy
Hitting bottom	The X factor

Obviously, these match-ups are not exclusive. All of the adult love traits will help you change all of your Wendy responses.

Give-and-Take

It is my contention that nature gave us a heart and a head designed more to *give* love than to *receive* it. Giving love comes naturally; accepting it takes work. That's why it's so sad that people don't permit themselves to do what comes naturally—give love.

Many people are slow to give love because they are afraid of the risks that accompany it. When giving love, we must lower our defenses and open our hearts. In doing so, we give ourselves the chance to be loved in return. However, we also open ourselves to disappointment and disapproval. The state of vulnerability that accompanies loving can be frightening, especially to those who have fears of rejection left over from younger days. Once you know how to hurt and recover, it is easier to be vulnerable and take the risk of getting hurt.

Give-and-take, as a part of the adult love script, helps a person open up so that not only can love get out, but another's love can also get in. As already suggested, give-and-take is especially applicable to a Wendy who's used to playing the martyr. Martyrs are wonderful at giving love but not nearly as good at taking it. Listen to a woman who used to give love continually, but put up shields to keep loving from coming in.

"Taking love made me feel guilty. I remember saying that I didn't deserve it. I'd try to find fault with my husband's love, saying he wasn't doing it right—anything, just to keep love away from my heart. Yet inside I was begging for it. I just didn't think I was good enough. You know what started me changing? Oh, it was a small thing, but big enough for me. I started saying 'thanks' when people complimented me. I didn't get all embarrassed like I used to and start saying something was wrong with me. I just smiled and said thanks. It felt real funny at first, but what a great start.

"I started saying thank-you to my friends, then to strangers, and once, when my husband heard me do it, he later asked me if I was all right. He had heard the difference but didn't know what it was. I then explained it to him and asked him to start paying me compliments again—he had stopped after not wanting to hear me cutting myself down. Now I say thanks to him. It feels great."

The simple act of permitting a compliment to get past the shields of protection can quickly lead to much more. It feels so good that you'll want more. That's when the spirit of loving will encourage you to ask your man for compliments.

Here's how Meghan (see Chapter 12), who made mountains out of molehills by blaming herself for everything that went wrong, took a small step toward accepting love from her man.

"I never let Patrick do anything around the house because I was convinced he would never do it right. Once I realized I was using my spotless house as a symbol of martyrdom, I took a small step—I asked him to help me scrub the floors. His reaction surprised me. He said, 'Sure.' And all that time I'd moaned about how he would never help me in the house. I was so busy feeling sorry for myself that I had never asked him. Men are sometimes quite ready to help. They just have to be asked."

Not all men react with Patrick's compliance and willingness. Many men, especially those who prefer to live in Never-Never Land, automatically assume that housework and child care are a woman's job. If a martyr has reinforced this notion through continual self-sacrifice, she may have to find an innovative solution to teach her man a new definition of give-and-take in the home. Here's how one woman did it:

"After confronting my martyr role, I knew things had to change in the daily routine around the house. I was doing everything for two healthy teenagers and a spoiled man. And I deserved a lot of the disrespect they gave me—not all of it—but a lot. I had nagged, left notes, and even lowered myself to screaming that they didn't love me. When I heard that come out of my mouth, I knew something had to give.

"Here's what I did. One evening I sat down and wrote on individual three-by-five cards every single thing I had done that day, no matter how small. One thing was written on each card. By the time I was finished, I had eighty cards, with such things on them as 'wiped off counter,' 'let dog out,' and 'took meat out of the freezer.' I was shocked at the number of things, many of them little, that I had done during the day. And that had been a slow day.

"The next morning I shuffled the deck of cards and, with a little grin, said to my husband, 'Pick two cards.' He looked at me as if I'd flipped out, but I just repeated, 'Pick two cards.' When he asked why, I replied, 'These are all the things I do around here. Whatever two things you pick, *you* are going to do today and the rest of this week, because I won't do them.' I did the same thing with the kids. This was my way of breaking the martyrdom trip I had been on. By the way, I don't have to use the cards anymore to get help."

Innovative solutions to kicking the martyrdom habit require that a woman give herself the right to expect love and consideration in return. The adult love script suggests that you shouldn't *demand* it, but you certainly must expect it. Once this woman stopped demanding it and martyring herself when that didn't work, she simply started expecting it.

Following through on such an assertion is the last hurdle to overcome in beginning to accept the giving from another person. Accomplishing this task also calls for innovative measures.

"I used to spend the entire day making sure my

man would adore his dinner. I chose to be a housewife, and since I overcame my martyrdom, I really
love it. However, my man didn't adjust too well. I
had to take some tough action.

"I told him that I wanted some compliments
about my dinner, and then I wanted us to clean up
together. I waited a few days, with no positive results. Then I simply found other things to do at the
dinner hour. I took a class at the junior college at
five P.M. and didn't get home until six-thirty. The
first few times, he was waiting for me, demanding
to know where dinner was. I said it was in the re-
frigerator and the cupboards. Poor guy thought I
had gone off my rocker. I prepared a late dinner,
asking him to compliment it. This time he did. He
also helped me clean up. If he hadn't given me some
consideration, I was ready to keep up the late din-
ners until he did."

Not only did this woman have to give herself the
right to expect some love in return, she actually had
to teach her man how to do it. This may sound as if
she was training a little boy to behave himself, but
in truth, she was following through on her expectation of positive strokes for her work. Remember,
there is nothing in the adult love script that says you
can't *help* your man become sensitive to your
needs. That help may involve step-by-step education. It's reassuring to realize that no one ever
taught him how to help around the house.

You've noticed that Tinker has a sense of humor.
She especially needs one if she is combating martyrdom. Here is a woman who used her sense of

humor to break the vicious cycle of self-pity that often feeds martyrdom.

"No matter what I tried to do for him, there always seemed to be this little voice inside of me saying, 'You poor baby, you never get back what you give.' It seemed I was always in the 'pity pit.' It was eating me alive. So I took a little humorous action on myself.

"Every time I felt myself falling into the pity pit, I went to my bathroom, looked at myself in the mirror, and repeated out loud, 'You poor thing, nobody appreciates you. Poor baby.' I kept repeating it until it sounded so silly I'd laugh. And the spell was broken. I could go on with my daily schedule without pity. Whenever that inner voice returned, I just went to the nearest bathroom and made fun of my pity. I'll tell you, you get some pretty strange looks from friends and family when you run to the bathroom all the time. I finally told my mom what I was doing. She looked at me like I was weird. But then, she should have been doing the same thing years ago."

Falling into the pity pit is a regular occurrence for a Wendy-becoming-a-Tinker. This woman found a humorous way of climbing out. She understood that she might have to battle self-pity on a daily basis for months to come. She thought that was fine; it was all part of growing up.

Tolerance and Empathy

Putting yourself into another's shoes without losing sight of what you believe is a task a mature person must accomplish. It calls for compassion, under-standing, and forgiveness, characteristics that are not compatible with the Wendy responses. Once you can cultivate some empathy for your man, you can tolerate some of his personality traits you don't like.

Empathy also gives you the ability to judge whether or not your man is trying to reciprocate.

"I can understand the pain my husband goes through on his job. His boss is not a nice man and his job is frustrating. I realize that and I feel for him. But that shouldn't give him the right to come home and take his frustrations out on me. Understanding goes just so far. Then I realize he isn't trying to be nice to me. He feels sorry for himself and thinks he has the right to be mean and inconsiderate to me. I'll have empathy for him if I see he's *trying to deal* with his frustrations, not just dumping them on me when he doesn't want them.

"When he tries to work through his own pain, I'm willing to tolerate his grumpiness. But if he doesn't, I just walk away. I don't totally understand what he's going through, but I sure don't have to stand around and take his abuse.

"If he doesn't take responsibility for his own stress, I just walk away. That seems to shake him. He tries to continue to browbeat me for a minute or two, but when I still won't fight, he usually calms down and eventually apologizes.''

Empathy and tolerance should not be confused with permitting oneself to be another's punching bag. A woman who accepts nastiness from her man tends to give it back in kind. That's why empathy and tolerance will help a woman get rid of her punishment response.

''I found myself giving him the same kind of cheap shots that I had come to expect from him. I knew I had to think more of myself than to permit that to happen. I couldn't control his anger, but I could mine. I decided I would simply get angry with him, being as honest as I could.

''Instead of making up excuses why I didn't want to have sex with him, I told him the truth. I said, 'You've been busy making war on me, and I don't want to make love with you.' It was hard to say at first. But I said to myself, 'I don't have to tolerate his nastiness when I know he's not trying.''

''Instead of making fun of him in front of others, I either walked away and drove myself home or else confronted him about what he had said or done at the moment it happened. The first time I did that, we were with friends, and I took him into another room and told him in short words without screaming what I was angry about. I was tempted to confront him in front of his friends, but I decided that I was too fine a person to sink that low. Other women say it works, but I don't want him if that's what I have to do.''

There are two other ways you can use the love

contained in tolerance and empathy to banish punishment from the way you relate to your man. They both involve forgiveness.

If you find that you have been a punisher, you'll need to forgive yourself. It's necessary before you can overcome your negative attitudes toward your man. But it can be a very difficult thing to do.

"Forgiveness is easy to say but tough to do, especially when I think that many of our problems could have been prevented if only I had come to my senses sooner. I tell myself, 'You're a good person and have the right to make mistakes.' That helps a lot. Whenever I find myself drifting back into punishment, I remove myself from the situation immediately. Then I give myself that little pep talk about making mistakes. The hardest part is accepting the fact that I can be so stupid. I guess tolerance works both ways."

Tolerance and empathy are traits that should guide you in loving yourself as well as your man. Some women find it easier to forgive their man's cruelty than to forgive the oversights they see in themselves. This is all part of the silent voice of inferiority (see Chapter 4).

If a Wendy is successful in forgiving herself, she can probably reduce the degree of her punishment immediately. With greater self-control, she might be able to exercise the second part of the forgiveness strategy. One woman put it this way:

"I knew there had to be a reason for the way my husband treated me. He wouldn't or couldn't tell me, and he wouldn't go and talk with anyone about it. And I wanted to know why.

"In order to figure it out, I had to get myself under control, which I did simply by walking away and refusing to let myself start punishing him.

"Then something strange happened. He came after me, taunting me, calling me names, almost daring me to punish him. Then it dawned on me. *He wanted me to punish him.* He expected it, like a mischievous boy caught stealing from his sister's piggy bank. It all seemed pretty simple to me. For whatever reasons, my husband felt as if he was being a bad boy around me. Heaven knows he had some reason to want to shape up. But that wasn't what he wanted. He wanted to be punished. As if punishment would make him feel okay again.

"Once I regained control of myself, I was able to confront him right in the middle of one of his taunting sessions. I didn't try to make him look small. I just waited until he paused and then I looked him squarely in the eye and said, 'Honey, I will not punish you. I'm not your mother. So if you can't talk sensibly about changes, please leave me alone.' "

This kind of rational confrontation requires a woman to have grown up a great deal. It will prove difficult for many women. And it may not work. When a woman changes her behavior patterns, she upsets the equilibrium between herself and her man. It's possible he won't be able to adjust. You'll find further information in Chapter 20 on what to expect when you change.

Dependability

A woman in love wants to be able to count on her man. She wants him to listen to her when she's down, be cheerful on a dreary day, help her clean the house when company's coming, and understand her moods. In short, she wants him to be there when she needs him.

A woman who mothers her man has to contend with his weaknesses and undependability as well as her own disappointment and bitterness. The adult love trait of dependability is often misused by the Wendy woman in that she is always there when her man needs her, even when he should stand on his own two feet. Attaining rational dependability is a tough thing for a Wendy to learn.

"I was always there when he needed me. I'd listen for hours as he complained about work and his boss. I would cancel plans I had made so that he wouldn't have to be alone at night. Yet he never seemed to be there when I needed him. I finally decided to keep track of his problems and see if he ever changed his complaints. He didn't.

"I knew I couldn't keep listening to him complain about his work. I wasn't helping him. So I told him that together we'd work out a strategy for confronting his boss. I took a piece of paper, listed all the complaints—I knew them by heart—and told him to think of all the things he could do: quit, scream at the boss, ask for a transfer, go to his boss's boss, prepare a formal complaint, have the boss to dinner, and so on.

"I handed him the list and asked him which one he could do first. He just shrugged his shoulders. I set my mind firmly and told him, 'If you don't start working on a solution, even something we haven't written down, I'm not going to listen to your complaints anymore.'

"One night he came home in a foul mood and started in again about his boss. When I learned that he had done nothing about working on his problem, I said, 'I don't want to hear it,' and walked away. It was a very hard thing to do.

"Later that night, I saw him in the den looking at the list and mumbling to himself. He still hasn't solved his work problem, but at least now he thinks it's *his* problem, not mine."

Overprotective women are usually quite competent at getting things done. They drive themselves to the edge doing six things at once. They are dependable to a fault. Backing off is tough but necessary. Here's how another woman decreased her overprotection but remained dependable.

"My man won't lift a finger to help me. He won't go shopping or help with the chores, and believe it or not, he forgot to pick up the kids from school one day when I was busy with my grandmother. When the teacher called me and said the kids were still there and my husband said he 'forgot,' I knew it was time for me to do something.

"I started by leaving his clothes scattered all over the house. Oh, I'd pile them in various corners to get them out of the way, but I didn't pick them up. When he asked for his tennis shorts, I pointed at a pile and said, 'Maybe you ought to check over there.' It took about two weeks of that before he started putting his clothes in the hamper.

"Then I started feeding the kids before he got home and told him he'd have to cook his own meals because I was on a diet. I would offer him some of my melba toast, but he would grumble and open a can of soup. It took only a week of that before he remembered to help me out by stopping at the grocery store on the way home from work.

"I really hated to have to do these things, but they worked. I called it 'going on strike for better working conditions.' He said I was growing fangs. We both laughed."

Backing off from overprotection will usually result in some type of guilt trip. As long as a woman knows she has tried the open, honest communication approach, free from nagging, she can feel confident that she is doing the rational thing.

One other rational thing that frees a Wendy from overprotection is increasing her own level of self-dependability. In some cases, the key to this strength is the ability to earn money.

"I didn't like being totally dependent upon my husband for all my spending money. It made me feel indebted to him. But I didn't have any really good skills. So I went to the local junior college and talked to a guidance counselor. I felt stupid until I discovered that there were hundreds of other women in my shoes.

"I made my career decision based on my interests, my past experiences, and my need for a short-term educational program. I settled on bookkeeping, not only because I could learn it at night, but also because I was doing an excellent job of managing all the household money.

"My husband couldn't understand why I was going back to school. He said he made plenty of money and I couldn't make enough to matter. His comments only strengthened my determination.

"I don't plan on getting a full-time job outside my home, but I feel more secure knowing that I could support myself if I had to. I believe it's helped our relationship. Because I feel stronger, I don't try to be such a Superwoman."

Financial insecurity is the one characteristic that affects most Wendy women; it crosses the boundaries of all the Wendy responses. We'll deal with it again later in this chapter.

Personal Development

Many people, men and women alike, have a tendency to stop pursuing personal development once they "settle down." One of the negative side effects of this stagnation is possessiveness. One woman broke free of her possessiveness by learning how to repossess herself.

"When I got married, I literally gave myself away. I didn't realize it until I saw myself becoming just as bitter and resentful as my mother. It took a long time before I figured out what was wrong.

"My husband went on a fishing trip and I cried the entire time he was gone. I blamed him for my misery. He was supposed to entertain me. I was sniveling like a baby.

"I finally looked at myself in the mirror and gave myself a swift kick in the pysche. It was time for me to get on with my life. So I went out and bought myself a jogging suit and a tennis racket and signed up at a health club. I vowed to do whatever I had to in order not to let myself drown in self-pity anymore."

Taking control of one's life is an essential ingredient for becoming a Tinker. You don't have to start jogging around the block or become an instant jock. In fact, there's no formula that spells out how any one individual learns to become more of a person. You can become the best you want to be without taking your lead from what others are doing or saying.

"My minister had been telling me I needed to have more self-respect. Unfortunately, I didn't understand what he meant. We talked about my career. I had always been told to be of service to others, and it seemed the best way to do that was to be a nurse. So I did it. It's okay, but I don't really enjoy it. I want something different.

"When he asked me what I would really like to do, I surprised myself by saying, 'Sell women's fashions.' When I asked him if I should do it, he said, 'You should do what is right for you.' I waited for him to give me permission to do what I wanted to. He told me that I was old enough to give myself permission. That really struck home.

"When I first announced my intention, my husband and friends thought I was crazy. I was hit with all the arguments—poor pay, giving up my chosen career, unsteady work—but I did it anyway. Once I explained to my husband that nursing was my *mother's* choice for me, not mine, he seemed to understand. Once he realized how much happier I was, he was all for my new job. He even helps out with the kids, something I never thought he would do."

This woman broke free from a restrictive role imposed upon her by her parents and social conditioning. She "repossessed" a part of her life that, through passivity, she had permitted someone else to control.

When a woman develops herself first as a person, she is free to choose what other roles she may wish to enact. She is not victimized by definitions of what she must be as a worker, or as a woman, or, for that matter, as a wife. If you are serious about becoming a Tinker, you will use my suggestions on loving as a springboard to personal development, not as a guide to roles you *must* enact.

Personal development will help you guard against the development of narcissism. As you'll recall from Chapter 9, narcissism can manifest itself in a woman when she seeks to blindly implement a rigid definition of femininity with the belief that it will somehow magically solve the problems of attracting and keeping a man. Susan Brownmiller's book *Femininity* (see Appendix) is an excellent resource for helping you redefine your role as a woman.

If you're not sure of where to start in developing yourself as a person, consider this woman's experience.

"I didn't know how to have an opinion. Oh, I knew how to say what I thought other people wanted to hear, and I certainly knew how to complain—just ask my husband. But I always thought of people who had opinions as opinionated, and I didn't want to be that way.

"When I learned that having an opinion can be a wonderful experience, I was hooked. I started practicing having opinions. It sounds silly, but when you don't know how to run, you first have to learn how to crawl.

"You should have seen me trying to decide what season of the year I liked; not what people told me I liked, but what *I* liked. After that, I thought about my preference in books, furniture, and even colors. I discovered that I had never learned how to think for myself.

"A whole new world opened up. It was a novelty for my husband until I started having opinions about politics and his friends. I became a person he'd never known before. I had to remember to slow down in order to give him a chance to adjust to the new me."

When a woman sees the futility in trying to control her man, she can turn her attention toward self-control. And as she learns to control herself, she takes possession of the attitudes, opinions, and values that guide her life. When she learns how to possess herself, she will no longer be possessive.

Sharing

"We have a problem communicating." Whenever there is trouble in a relationship, this statement is inevitably used to summarize the difficulty. It usually means that the two people involved confound and contaminate the sharing of thoughts and feelings. Wendy guards her words, not wishing to offend her hypersensitive Peter Pan. Peter, on the other hand, does his best to hide his emotions and avoid the truth, fearing that he will be responsible for hurting his fragile little woman.

Wendy's sharing with Peter Pan is stilted and overcontrolled. Since she is lacking in self-possession, she is worried about saying the wrong thing at the wrong time. She censors her sharing.

Tinker, on the other hand, speaks her mind. In fact, she can get so excited about sharing that she goes to the opposite extreme by overwhelming her partner with information. One can quickly overlook the excess, because she's on the right track.

Sharing is the most important attribute in the adult love script. Without the sharing of thoughts and feelings, a man and woman have little if any hope of forming the basis of a lasting commitment. In order to be effective, this sharing must occur in a nonjudgmental atmosphere. If one or both partners in a love relationship retains an air of superiority over the other, revenge and rebellion will infiltrate any attempt at sharing.

Below are three examples of how nonjudgmental

sharing can offset the overtones of control that often creep into a Wendy's relationship with a Peter Pan.

PSYCHOLOGIZING. "You know you're only upset because your mother paid more attention to your sister than you." This judging Wendy is guilty of psychologizing as she and her man "share" thoughts and feelings about a family reunion that turned sour. Whether or not her assessment is correct is beside the point. She was telling him how he felt and why. If he has trouble identifying and communicating his feelings, this type of mind reading is sure to result in further alienation.

If you are a Wendy-becoming-a-Tinker, you'll benefit from these two alternatives to psychologizing.

One way to tap his feelings about his family would be to convert the statement into a question. Specifying a situation is an excellent introduction. For example, "How did it make you feel when your mother ignored your news about your promotion in order to ask your sister about her new shoes?"

If he has a history of censoring his feelings and you have reacted by psychologizing, chances are he will avoid your question: "Oh, it didn't mean anything to me. That's the way it's always been." And you may be tempted to lapse back into mind reading: "C'mon, honey, I saw you turn red. You could've strangled somebody."

If questions don't work and you're dying to tell him your opinion, share it in such a way that you minimize any hint of accusation. "I know I felt angry at your mother for slighting you, and I guess I thought you did too.'' You know you can't drag emotions out of another person; your best chance to help is to share your feelings in the most honest way possible, encouraging your man to follow suit.

''YOU MESSAGES''   Many potentially profitable opportunities for sharing are sabotaged by the misuse of the word *you*. It occurs as an extension of the psychologizing noted above. ''You won't tell me what you're feeling,'' ''You like to see me squirm,'' and ''You just never grew up'' are inappropriate, judgmental ''you messages,'' destined to destroy meaningful sharing.

Employ ''I messages'' instead of ''you messages.'' When using ''I messages,'' try your best to avoid using *you* as the subject of a sentence. This is how the above statements would sound if *you* were replaced with *I*. ''I feel left out when I don't know or understand your feelings.'' ''I feel very uncomfortable when I'm the only one sharing my feelings.'' ''I get angry at you when I feel that I'm the only one of us trying to grow up.''

Converting ''you messages'' into ''I messages'' is something all partners in a love relationship can work on. If you and your man agree to work on this, just understand that your goal is unattainable—to eliminate entirely the pronoun *you* as the subject of a sentence in which personal sharing takes place. You'll probably never attain the ideal—100 percent efficiency—but the more you do it, the better your chances for nonjudgmental sharing.

* * *

CONFLICT RESOLUTION   Conflict in a love relationship is inevitable. Insofar as it gives both parties the chance to improve their ability to learn from mistakes, conflict is good. Here's how one woman described her experience with my suggestion for conflict resolution. She had sought help for improving her marriage; her husband had refused to come with her.

"I must admit that I thought your description of conflict as a pile of manure was somewhat silly. But the more I thought about it, the more sense it made to look at problems between me and my husband as so much crap stinking up our relationship.

"It also made a lot of sense to realize that I can only be responsible for my part of the manure pile. I explained the idea to my husband, and he, of course, thought it was stupid. I followed through with it anyway.

"We had this silly argument about how to make tacos. You told me to practice your suggestion with a small problem first—and believe me, this was a small problem. Anyway, my husband eats at a taco stand and is convinced he knows the perfect way to make them. I bought flat taco shells that you fry before eating. He told me that was a dumb thing to do, that it didn't make them taste any better. I couldn't believe he could be so pigheaded and I told him so. We had a gigantic fight.

"Later, I felt so foolish. So I did what you suggested. Without sounding like a guilty little girl, I simply said, 'That fight over tacos was a bunch of crap. And I want to own my share of it. I shouldn't have made such a big deal out of frying the shells first.'

"He didn't know what to say. He just looked at me. I explained that I was practicing owning my part of the manure pile—something I was learning in counseling. He still didn't say a word. Boy, did I want to tell him what his part of the manure was, but I didn't.

"You said it would be hard to own my part of the pile without him owning his. This had better work, because I don't like me taking all the crap and him taking none."

The Tinker takes responsibility for her contribution to the conflict—owns her part of the manure pile—without forcing her man to follow suit. She demonstrates mature, self-possessed behavior in the hope that she is setting an example her man will emulate. As you will learn in Chapter 21, if her man does not eventually reciprocate, the Tinker will not continue unilateral acceptance of responsibility without seriously considering the alternative of leaving. Nonjudgmental sharing is a critical element of a productive love relationship. However, if sharing becomes a one-way street, love is destined to reach a dead end.

Realism

The lesson expressed by this attribute of the adult love script is simple. *Lovers cause themselves unnecessary stress by expecting to resolve 100 percent of all conflicts.* Young lovers are exceptionally vulnerable to the notion that love demands unanimity in all matters of daily living. A sense of reality would help them balance their desire to be of one mind with the practicality that some conflicts just aren't resolvable.

This understanding leads to the prioritizing of problems according to their overall impact on the relationship. Arguments about tacos need not be resolved (other than each owning his or her responsibility for the fight), while time and energy invested in resolving child-rearing differences have long-term payoffs. Certain issues may not be important to one partner, but are to the other. Give-and-take and sharing must both be employed if the lovers are to reach a consensus on the issues to be worked on and those to be allowed to fade into history.

As the lovers adopt a sense of reality, denial decreases and honest self-disclosure increases. Reality can be very painful for a Wendy to encounter, especially if she realizes that, although she is trying to eliminate inappropriate mothering, her man is steadfastly refusing to return from Never-Never Land. The pursuit of realism can lead a woman to the inescapable conclusion that her love is going nowhere and it may be time to get out.

However, for the vast majority of lovers, it is a healthy, freeing experience to accept the reality that a 70-percent relationship is a marvelous achievement. Allow me to explain.

Think back over the past couple of weeks of your relationship. Consider each and every interaction, even if that interaction was the exchange of a nonverbal glance. Then ask yourself how many of those interactions were essentially positive. If seven out of every ten interactions was characterized by warmth, playfulness, understanding, and kindness, then you have a 70-percent love relationship—a fantastic basis upon which to build even greater love.

Intimacy

Lovers love to touch, hug, kiss, hold hands, and freely express erotic pleasures with each other. Within their intimacy is plenty of room for playfulness.

Since 80 percent of sexuality occurs *above* the shoulders (if the pleasure centers in your brain are disturbed, sexuality will be filled with disappointment), sexual intimacy has more to do with the way lovers touch each other's soul than how they fondle each other's body.

Here are two reactions to suggestions for improved intimacy given to women who were being counseled by my wife, Nancy.

"When you first suggested that we needed to do more together than worry about bills and complain about the kids, I thought it would be easy to come up with something. But it wasn't.

"I racked my brain until I realized there must be a way to put our separate interests into one venture. I am really excited to learn about antiques and my husband loves his gun collection. So I suggested we go to an antique auction. He could look for old guns and I could search for my first purchase.

"Well, we both got hooked on the auction and fell in love with an antique gun case. It was painted an awful green but we decided to bid on it. Another person wanted it and we were on pins and needles until we won.

"We've already spent hours figuring out the best way to restore it, and my husband went out and bought all the stuff we need. He is really excited about putting his guns in the case, and I think it'll make a great addition to the family room furniture.

"Most important, we've had so much fun doing this together that he wants to buy more antiques. He even saw a four-poster pine bed for our bedroom."

The special intimacy that took place on this nonerotic level nourished this couple's relationship more than all the sex counseling in the world could have. The spirit of togetherness was rekindled in such a way that it would naturally lead to more erotic sharing.

There is a psychological lesson contained in this story that deserves special mention. This woman had been advised to encourage her husband to get involved in some type of artistic endeavor. He was technically oriented, not easily given to involvement in arts and crafts. She had been given this recommendation because research suggests that the walls people erect to keep each other at arms' length tend to dissolve in a situation where art supersedes technology. She had been encouraged to find an activity involving music, dance, painting, or any other endeavor where her husband could express his inner feelings without the restraints imposed by technology. Expressing one's artistic talents, however limited, can often be the first step toward an increase in intimacy.

The second woman capitalized on her own feelings of sexual need by becoming quietly aggressive.

"As you know, I felt as if I was losing Jack to the health club. He always goes there after work, plays himself into exhaustion, and then, after dinner, falls asleep on the couch.

"I decided to do something daring; complaining sure wasn't working.

"On a night when he was working late and wouldn't get to the club, I created a special spa in our bathroom. Bubble bath, champagne, and a tray of munchies. When I told him to undress, he looked at me as if I'd lost my mind. But he did it.

"I motioned him into the tub and started rubbing his neck. Then I climbed into the tub with him. It was a tight fit. We drank the bubbly, ate munchies, and started throwing water at each other.

"We both got chilled and jumped into bed. I rubbed his back with oil, and well, one thing led to another, and we had the best lovemaking ever."

Needless to say, this approach doesn't always work out so perfectly. If you try it and your man proves unreceptive or too demanding, back off as soon as you feel yourself becoming frustrated. Explain that your mood is not "clicking" with his and that you need to take a break. Breaking off the playfulness before bitterness wells up inside prevents building up and storing further negative feelings.

The X factor

Lovers recognize that there is an unspoken bond between them. It is a special feeling of closeness and is unnamed and indefinable; hence the label, the X factor.

Rather than comment any further on this special attribute of the adult love script, allow me to summarize the comments of one young woman who was pinning her hopes on the X factor.

"My mother has been a Wendy for over thirty years and I know I often act just like her. I hate it when I fall into the trap of mothering my husband. But he can act like such a baby. And I'm not aware of what's going on until it's too late.

"There's a very thin line between loving and mothering. And when I'm feeling insecure, I know darn well that I cross over into mothering. He has this habit of blaming me for everything that goes wrong. When I'm feeling good about myself, I don't take his bait. But when I'm down, I start feeling guilty and then I start mothering.

"I get real confused about a lot of things. But I know one thing for sure. I love him and I'm not going to throw that away. And don't ask me to say why I love him. I just know I do. And to me, love is not some silly emotion—it is a commitment to give to another person. I'm going to keep giving and keep loving because I know that he loves me. He's just never learned how to show it. And I believe that someday my giving will pay off.

"I don't want love from another man, I want *his* love. I will not accept the fact that he can't learn to love me. I will not accept it."

I do not know this woman's husband. But I sincerely hope he wakes up before he loses the most precious gift that life has to offer—the dedicated commitment of another human being.

18

Practicing the Tinker Response

"I had to learn to take it one step at a time. After all, I was learning something new, and you can't do that overnight."

To refresh your memory, Tinker was a gutsy little ball of light, assertive to the point of aggressiveness. She snipped at people's hair and, when someone behaved in an irrational manner, called them a "silly ass." To call her self-possessed is an understatement; "possessed" is more like it—possessed with a spirit of freedom and adventure. But even Tinker had a few things to learn. She needed to refine her self-assertion and stop trying so hard to be liberated.

Once they recognize their Wendy, many women go to the opposite extreme and try to become a Tinker overnight. They realize that one of the reasons they fell into the Wendy trap was that they blindly accepted a restrictive role definition of what a woman was supposed to be. In their disgust with society in general and themselves in particular, they seek to learn a new role by defining themselves as liberated women or feminists. They absorb everything they can about this new role and enact it with dispatch. But all is not well. There is still a yearning inside of them. Why? Because in their haste, they have only exchanged one restrictive role for another. They call themselves liberated but are still imprisoned by the definition imposed upon them by someone outside themselves.

When you become a Tinker, you *slowly define yourself.* You resist the imposition of behaviors that you are "supposed" to enact. Because you have quieted your voice of inferiority, you're no longer panicked by the possibility of disapproval. You take your time in experimenting with new behaviors, selecting those roles you feel comfortable with. You are free to pick and choose among endless ways of behaving. Best of all, you are free to change, grow, and modify your actions as you see fit. The gradual emergence of the Tinker within you is the most effective way to stop mothering without abandoning your love.

This chapter will help you practice your Tinker response. Because it is important that you do so at your own time and speed, I will focus my recommendations on your individual lifestyle, without reference to men. I will review techniques that will help you modify your attiudes and behavior. You're undoubtedly acquainted with most of these, so I won't bore you with excessive details. The books recommended in the Appendix will aid your understanding if my explanations here are insufficient.

As you consider each of these techniques, be advised that I have added a special emphasis to each one. It may not always be apparent, but these techniques have been redesigned to insure that you take better care of yourself. The Wendy within you may dissent, saying, "You're just being self-centered." Actually, she's right. But I happen to think that being self-centered is not a bad thing. If self-centered sounds too much like selfish (which I think *is* a bad thing), then call my suggestions self-promoting.

The suggestions contained in this chapter are founded upon a philosophy of "moralistic self-promotion." Moralistic self-promotion is my answer to the unbridled narcissism dominating much of our culture. It is a middle-of-the-road philosophy that guards against the extremes of hedonism (where your ego is given no self-discipline) and psychological fascism, in which your ego is permitted no room for individual expression.

The moralistic self-promoter gives unselfishly to those who she thinks will appreciate it. She knows that this is the best avenue for receiving love. However, if hurt, she turns her cheek but once. To a nonintimate person, she practices the philosophy "Fool me once, shame on you; fool me twice, shame on me."

The self-promoter is a firm believer in the golden rule. She gives herself the right to be wrong. She enjoys pleasurable pursuits, balancing the passions of the present with the needs of the future. She avoids extremes in all matters, maintains her behavior within the laws affecting the common good, and enjoys the serenity of a spiritual life based on an educated conscience.

If you feel comfortable with this philosophy, you can confidently explore the recommendations that flow from it. You can use the recommendations to take better care of yourself. As I'm sure you've heard before, if you can't be good to yourself, you won't be good for anyone else.

HUMOR

One of the strongest indicators of mental health is a sense of humor. Being able to find a silver lining in the biggest cloud is an essential ingredient to having a positive outlook on life. No matter how deeply ensnared in the Wendy trap you might be, you need to find something to laugh about (chuckle, at least). A sense of humor is so critical that, in my opinion, you cannot make lasting changes in your life without it. I put humor first on the list of recommended techniques because, without it, the rest of the suggestions won't work.

All of the terminology in this book—Wendy, Tinkerbell, Peter Pan, and Never-Never Land—lends itself to the lighter side of self-evaluation. Using humor to take yourself less seriously is not the same as suppressing your problems with a giggle. In fact, being able to laugh at yourself gives you the opportunity to gain a better perspective on your difficulties, thereby making it more likely that you'll implement effective remedial procedures.

The most therapeutic way to employ humor is to

use it in conjunction with paradoxical intention. Some might call it "reverse psychology." For example, if your Wendy likes to mother your friends, exaggerate your behavior to the point of silliness. Let's say you catch yourself telling your friend how to do something that she's perfectly capable of doing (write out a check, talk to someone on the phone). Stop yourself in mid-mothering and say, "Now, little girl, this is your mother talking. Of course you don't know how to do that simple thing. If you listen to me, you will always do it right. And we all know that mother knows best." The intention of your behavior has been exaggerated to such a paradoxical extreme that you demonstrate to yourself the inefficiency of inappropriate mothering.

RELAXATION

The goal of relaxation is to rid your body of tension so that oxygen can flow freely to all parts of your body, most especially your brain. If your body is relaxed and your brain is working at an optimum level, you have a better chance of taking control of your life. The three essential ingredients of effective relaxation are: proper breathing, muscle awareness, and thought control.

If you're facing an anxiety-provoking situation (getting a child into college, or asking for a raise), a simple relaxation procedure can reduce your anxiety.

Begin by taking an "oxygen cocktail." A couple of deep breaths, each held for a couple of seconds, will bring a comfortable shot of oxygen into your system. If you form your mouth into the shape of an *O* and breathe slowly, you will be able to listen to the sound of your own breathing.

This sound will encourage you to get your mind off whatever you're worrying about, if only for a few seconds, and lead you to muscle awareness. As you breathe, you'll become aware of your chest muscles tightening and relaxing as they expand and contract. The butterflies in your stomach created by anxiety can be set free by becoming aware of relaxing your diaphragm muscles. You can generalize this exercise to any set of muscles you wish, tightening and relaxing.

As you become aware of your muscles, it will be easier to channel your thoughts into willful control over the amount of tension in your body. The key to thought control is concentration. If you focus your attention on breathing and muscle relaxation, you can literally "talk" to your muscles, just as you did when communicating with yourself during psycho drama. This procedure is clarified in Dr. Herbert Benson's book *The Relaxation Response* (see Appendix).

The trick in using relaxation is to identify anxiety as soon as it appears. The insight "I'm nervous" should be followed by the self-directive "Take a deep breath." The more you establish this connection in your mind, the more control you will gain over your anxiety. One common mistake many people make when implementing a relaxation procedure is to attempt to "command" the body to relax.

The body rebels against such authoritarianism. Rather than inducing relaxation, such commands tend to increase tension, thereby frustrating the entire procedure.

You will have a much better chance of relaxing if you give yourself "permission" to let go of tension. Thus, after taking a deep breath and becoming aware of your muscles, tell yourself to let go of the tension instead of commanding the tension to leave. Properly induced relaxation procedures will remind you to move slowly in selecting how you wish to actualize your Tinker response.

THOUGHT LISTING

Thought listing is a simple but highly effective procedure for monitoring your Wendy responses as well as guiding the development of your Tinker response. When you first practice thought listing, select a situation that is multifaceted and relatively unemotional. Shopping is an excellent choice. You will have many different thoughts to monitor no matter what kind of shopping expedition you undertake.

When you return from the selected activity, take a few minutes from your schedule to list the thoughts you remember having. In this case, feelings also count as thoughts; list them as well. Don't worry about recalling all your thoughts; if you don't remember one, it will come back to you again.

Keep all your lists in a section of a private diary. When you have a few moments to reflect, review your lists of thoughts and notice ones that are repeated. The repetition of thoughts and feelings can tell you something about the direction your life is taking or the direction you want it to take. Thus, if a feeling of being under pressure seems to repeat itself, there may be something in your life that needs changing. If your thoughts often stray to moving or getting a new job, then a critical evaluation of your daily lifestyle is needed. Maybe you worry constantly about your children; altering your parenting style should be considered.

Thought listing is a quick, easy way of taking stock of your life. Although it won't give you direct relief, it may point you in the direction you need to go. This can be invaluable.

THOUGHT STOPPING

If you discover that certain unpleasant or unproductive thoughts are invading your daily life, you can use a simple procedure to stop them. Thought stopping involves the willful intrusion of overt self-instruction (see the section on this later in the chapter) for the purpose of interrupting the progression of thought.

It works this way: You're driving in the car, on your way to a social gathering. Your voice of inferiority combines with your worry about social approval to give rise to the persistent thought "What if they don't like me?" It is important to replace this negative thought with a positive one. However, before you can do that, the negative one must be stopped. A quick way to stop the thought is to say out loud, "Stop." You make an overt statement indicating what you wish your brain to do. From the psychodramatic perspective, your Tinker is telling your Wendy to be quiet. (This is *not* the same as telling Wendy to go away.)

Saying "stop" out loud is very effective. It will interrupt the progression of your thought pattern. And you can continue to use thought stopping as often as you feel comfortable saying, even whispering, "stop" overtly. However, thought stopping alone will not erase a negative thought from your mind. You'll need to replace the negative thoughts with a positive one: "I'm a likable person. Some will like me, some won't. I will simply be me; that's all I can do." When used together, thought listing, thought stopping, and overt self-instruction give you the opportunity to alter the course of your thinking.

TAPE-RECORDING

It may be embarrassing for a person to listen to his or her voice on tape. But to the woman who wishes to check herself for a Wendy response, it is very helpful. The challenge of using this technique is the cumbersomeness of the needed equipment. Yet if you avail yourself of every possible opportunity, you will find many chances to tape your voice. Record a business meeting, your part of a phone conversation (don't forget to tell the friend what you're doing), a friend's visit, or general conversation when you're relaxing around home. The only precaution is to protect your privacy.

Treat your tape recordings as you do your diary. They are to be used for a constructively critical look at your verbal behavior. If you invite an intimate to help you listen for Wendy responses, you should be 99 percent certain that he or she will not betray your confidence. It is immensely helpful to form a team with such a person, each willing to help the other evaluate his or her respective behavior.

Other guidelines for using this technique include: Listen for "power" words and phrases; for example, "He lets me," "What will I do with him?" "How can I make him . . . ?" Pay attention to voice qualities that make you sound ominous or scared. Compare certain repetitious phrases with the thoughts listed in your diary, noting similarities that may indicate ideas you need to examine further. If you save certain tapes for additional review, put them in a private place. Don't use your tape recordings to cavesdrop on other persons. If you ever visit a counselor, make sure to tape and save all conversations; revicwing the sessions will help you get your money's worth.

THE GARLOCK GAMBIT

There are tens, if not hundreds, of books on self-assertion. Some of the books listed in the Appendix provide guidance on this complicated subject. In this section I will give you some suggestions that have grown out of years of work with women who needed help with self-assertion. These techniques were designed by my wife, Nancy Garlock Kiley, in her work as a psychological counselor with women. Because they promote a favorable posture for you within an interpersonal power struggle, I group them under the heading "The Garlock Gambit." I strongly recommend that the Garlock Gambit *not* be used in any interaction with an intimate friend, husband, or lover.

The keystone of the most universal Garlock Gambit is to take control at the beginning of an interaction by making a statement that immediately puts you in a win-win situation. For example, when you are returning merchandise and expect some difficulty, you can maximize your chances of success by using this gambit: "Do you want to credit my account or give me the cash?" You have given the other person an opportunity to save face while you have increased your chances of getting what you want. Best of all, you can smile all the while.

The win-win gambit can be used in mildly confrontative situations, but save the following gambit for situations in which you are being treated gruffly. "Then what you're saying, sir (madam), is that your position leaves me no alternative. You are forcing me to lose my integrity." This must be said sternly and with mild indignation. This gambit is a calculated use of the tendency of most people to feel guilt. One of the problems with this underhanded strategy is that the user may feel guilty in trying to make the other person feel guilty. This gambit should be reserved for situations in which the insensitivity of the other person suggests that he or she deserves to be pulled down a peg or two.

A third dimension of the Garlock Gambit involves the judicious use of a misleading question. It must be used exactly as stated and you must be prepared to enter into an extended conversation in which confusion will reign. Notice how your request can be buried in this psuedo-question: "Don't you want to give me my money?" If the person says no, then you can say, "Good, I'm glad we agree." If he or she says yes, you can reply, "Excellent, that makes me feel good." There is no way to logically answer this so-called question. No matter what the response, you can select the interpretation you want.

The Garlock Gambit is a "game" insofar as you are not being perfectly open and honest about your wishes. *Warning*: The use of the gambit should be saved for situations in which self-promotion is actually self-protection.

OVERT SELF-INSTRUCTION

In *The Power of Positive Thinking*, Dr. Norman Vincent Peale says, "Whenever a negative thought concerning your personal powers comes to mind, deliberately voice a positive thought to cancel it out." In his textbook *Cognitive Psychology*, Dr. Donald Meichenbaum gives explicit instructions for the technique of overt self-instruction. (See Appendix for references.) Although these two authors differ in theoretical orientation, they are giving essentially the same advice. Overt self-instruction is the refined version of the power of positive thinking.

You can use overt self-instruction in many ways. Here is the way you use it to offset your silent voice of inferiority: When you find yourself in a situation in which you feel intimidated, the voice of inferiority has been activated. It says, "I'm not good enough to handle this problem." You counteract by saying, "I'm a good person and I will give this situation my best shot." Sounds too simple, right? Well, it is simple, *except* that you must say the positive thought *out loud*, and often.

Timing is the biggest obstacle in overt self-instruction. It works best if you give yourself an overt instruction just prior to beginning the encounter. Tell yourself that you are a good person just as you are about to answer the phone, enter a room, meet a new person, begin a difficult meeting, or start a conversation. The more you use overt self-instruction, the less you'll have to say it overtly. As the positive statement becomes a habit, it will work even when you say it silently.

You can test the power of overt self-instruction at any time. Now, for instance. Simply look away from this book and say aloud, "I'm a good person and deserve to be happy." You'll notice an immediate surge of warmth within you. Say it again and notice how you feel. The power you experience comes from affirming your essential goodness. You will double the effect if you practice relaxation and overt self-instruction simultaneously.

The beauty of overt self-instruction is that it is simple, yet powerful. The difficulty is that it calls for you to engage in a simplistic, childlike activity. But that is necessary. Remember, your voice of inferiority was conditioned when you were a child. The counterconditioning of overt self-instruction must be simple and childlike. When you say you are good, you are talking to the scared little girl inside you. You must use simple language she will understand.

SILENCE

Silence may be the most potent self promoting technique. It is by far the most difficult to employ. Its actual implementation is simpler than overt self-instruction; yet it can have a far-reaching impact on others. Depending upon the circumstances, it can be seen as exceptionally aggressive. If not used carefully, it can cause you trouble.

Imagine yourself sitting at a table with a group of women. The conversation is centered on the antics of the opposite sex. One of your acquaintances, in a spirit of mild sarcasm, looks directly at you and says, "Boy, can your guy be childish. Why, the other night at dinner, he was trying to make people laugh by making those silly sounds. Didn't you just want to slap him?"

Let's say that your instant reaction is that the woman has gone too far with her comment. But all the other women are waiting for your comeback, and you're not sure what to do. The most difficult thing to do at that moment, yet the one with the greatest impact, would be to look squarely into the woman's eyes, tilt your head slightly to one side, and with a blank expression say nothing. The silence would speak a thousand words, all of them saying the same thing: "That was a dumb thing to say." This use of silence can easily be interpreted as an act of aggression. At the very least, it will add a chill to any conversation. If and when you employ silence as an interpersonal strategy, it's a good idea not to let it last too long. In the above situation, five seconds of cold silence will seem like a lifetime. You can get your point across if you follow up such silence by ameliorating the tension. For example, say, "My man has a right to be silly without me wanting to slap him." A small dash of humor ("Anyway, standing him in the corner is a better punishment") will soothe any ruffled feathers. When used this way, silence breaks the momentum of this type of conversation and permits you to point it in a new direction.

A more moderate use of silence might be simply not to answer a pesky salesperson or an overzealous clerk. Punctuating your silence with a certain expression in your eyes is a good way to get your point across. A shrug of your shoulders and that "beats me" look are also helpful. Anxiety will provoke the other person to moderate his or her posture, allowing you to redirect the conversation. Silence is also an excellent tool to be used with a bothersome relative.

ACTIVE IGNORING

Active ignoring is another form of self-assertion. It has many of the same characteristics as silence. It is used to redirect a conversation, can be seen as aggressive, and is quite effective within the proper context. Active ignoring is, in truth, a strategic way of changing the subject. It has many areas of application, from pushy strangers to meddlesome relatives.

Let's go back to the conversation considered in the last section. If you'd like to be more subtle in responding to the sarcasm, this is how you'd employ active ignoring: Once the woman finishes her statement, give her a two-second, gentle look, then turn your attention to another person in the group and say, "You know, this food is not bad." Obviously, any general comment directed at another person gets the message across.

By actively ignoring an undesirable comment, you have said, in effect, "I will not dignify that statement with a reaction." If you have a history of weakness in self-assertion, then active ignoring, coupled with humor, might be an excellent way to seek improvement. However, when you begin to promote yourself, your friends and acquaintances may not understand. They may even see your assertion as an indication that something is troubling you. A review of Chapter 20 will help you understand their confusion.

SELF-HELP GROUPS

The techniques reviewed in this chapter are designed to strengthen your Tinker response. As stated, you can implement them with little or no help from another person. However, there is another self-promoting technique that is becoming increasingly important in the modern world. It takes its energy from the added strength of promoting yourself within a group where each member is pursuing a similar course. That technique is active participation in a self-help group.

Joining a self-help group can mean the difference between just reading or talking about changing your life and actually doing it. A group of people (usually seven to twelve), all dedicated to the same goal you are, has a dynamism that is greater than the sum of its parts. Members of a self-help group help each other set specific goals and overcome obstacles. Their regular meetings are filled with up-to-date information, encouragement, and constructive criticism. Best of all, the members share your pain and turmoil, offering empathy and support.

Besides attending the first meeting, the most difficult part of joining a self-help group is finding the one that best suits your needs and time restrictions. You'll have to do some research in order to find the best group for you. Your local community fund-raising organization (United Way, Community Chest, Crusade of Mercy, etc.) is an excellent place to start. Call and ask about self-help groups in your area. A trip through the Yellow Pages can also turn up other organizations that may have self-help groups. The local "Y" is a good resource. If all else fails, there is the Self-help Center in Evanston, Illinois; (312) 328-0470. The people there help you identify the kind of group you may need, as well as give you further hints on how to find it in your area.

You will most likely get the phone number of a prominent group member. Don't be disheartened if, when you call, you get a recorded message. Leave your name and number. When you talk to a member of the group, feel free to ask any question you want. If you decide to attend a group meeting, ask to accompany the person you called. Once you walk through the door, you'll be surprised how quickly you will feel at home. You needn't participate until you are ready. Once you start talking, all your worries will fade. If the meeting doesn't work, you can always congratulate yourself for trying, rest a few days, and try again.

The recommendations contained in the last chapter help you break free of the mothering trap. The techniques in this chapter help you rid yourself of the reason you started mothering in the first place. The self-promoting qualities of these techniques can help you get credit for your suggestions, assume a leadership role, refine and achieve your career goals, say no without feeling guilty, feel better about yourself in all respects, and, last but not least, realize a greater sense of participation in life.

Implement these recommendations slowly. Use the books listed in the Appendix to further augment your self-promotion. As was suggested in the last chapter's section on personal development, a key to self-promotion is some degree of financial independence. If the last chapter helped you feel more confident in your ability to love, I hope this chapter helped you feel you have a right to earn money— and to do so without guilt. There's absolutely no reason why you can't have plenty of love and lots of money. Moralistic self-promotion points the way.

19

Starting a Relationship on the Right Track

"I was in love with the idea of falling in love. I had to grow up a lot before I could tell the difference between an affair and a relationship."

Thousands of unattached women share a similar experience: they date a man four or five times, have a delightful time, feel very hopeful about the possibility of a long-lasting relationship, and, with little or no warning, never hear from the man again. The last thing they remember him saying is, "I'll call you next week." Some of the women are angry; all of them are confused. They complain, "Men are afraid of making a commitment to a relationship." They can't help searching their memory for what went wrong. Even though they may be quite mature, they can't resist the temptation to wonder what *they* did wrong.

They may not have done anything wrong, unless you consider being an incurable romantic a short-coming. However, more often than not, their mistake is working too hard at finding someone to fall in love with. Many women believe, as Dr. Penelope

Russianoff would say, they are nothing without a man.

Many women fall into the Wendy trap by picking the sweet fruit of love before it has had time to ripen. The lingering uncertainty of romance is unsettling. They are driven by their unresolved dependency needs to find someone who loves them. In their haste to find security, they force an encounter or an affair into becoming a relationship before the time is right. In so doing, they unwittingly communicate to the man a sense of urgency. They are in a hurry to find a special arrangement that will protect them from rejection. In her own way, the Wendy is also afraid of an adult commitment. By blaming the man, she loses sight of her ability to resolve the problem.

The Tinker is not panicked by the uncertainty of romance. She truly believes that her best opportunity to find a lasting relationship is to *not* work so hard to find it. This is the key to starting a relationship on the right track. Holly's story is a case in point.

Holly had been a Wendy for twenty years. She had served her man with unwavering dedication. She absorbed his rampant chauvinism without a word of complaint. Her "hitting bottom" experience centered on her children. She saw ample evidence that her thirteen-year-old son was following in her husband's footsteps. With considerable anguish and counseling, Holly got a divorce.

Holly was forty-five years old when she moved into an apartment with her two teenagers. Her office job, along with child support, gave her barely enough money to meet monthly bills. There was no room in her budget for the trips to the beauty salon, the tennis club, or her favorite clothing store. But Holly was bound and determined to break free of the restrictions that had kept her in bondage. Change was slow and painful; she had over forty years of conditioning to overcome. She craved a healthy love relationship, but she would not give up her freedom in exchange for a man.

Holly met several men whom she found attractive. She dated them, slept with them, and when they started behaving like little boys, dumped them. After several months of this experience, she decided that looking for a man wasn't worth the hassle. She was very content with her new life and not upset with the conclusion that she probably would never marry again. After all, it was a popular opinion that men wanted younger, more attractive women who would cater to their childish needs. Her independence was much too precious to throw away. It took a few extra years, but Holly had become a Tinker. Then, when she wasn't looking, she met Greg. He had recently been divorced. After twenty-five years of marriage, he wasn't too anxious to have a serious relationship. He realized that he had some growing up to do. He and Holly hit it off. On their first date, they made a pact that neither of them would try to control the other. They had long talks about how unrealistic control had destroyed their first marriages.

It wasn't long before they had opportunities to practice their arrangement. When Holly had problems with her ex-husband, Greg wanted to call him up and tell him to leave her alone. Holly politely but firmly told Greg that she would handle her ex-husband; he apologized. When Greg complained that the launderers were ironing wrinkles into his shirts, Holly said she would take them home and do them the correct way. Greg gave her a peck on the cheek as he reminded her that he could handle his own shirts; Holly apologized.

Greg and Holly gained mutual respect for each other. They achieved a level of understanding and communication that most couples never reach. They learned a very important lesson: *how to depend upon each other without becoming dependent.*

They still don't remember at what point they reached the same conclusion: They were in love. They were understandably cautious in disclosing their feelings. They didn't realize what was happening because neither of them had ever known adult love. It was an overwhelming experience for both of them. They were grown up, but felt like children. They knew how to go hand-in-hand to Never-Never Land and enjoy themselves; and then, when it was time to deal with reality, they knew how to come back.

Holly's comment contains an important lesson for all would-be Tinkers. "I don't believe what has happened to me. Just when I started learning how to rely on myself and live without a man, I discover love."

If you are currently "unattached," but are interested in having a love relationship, you should know that a Tinker isn't just sitting around, waiting

for love to drop into her life. She must work at
controlling her own destiny. When she frees herself
from hiding behind unrealistic control of another
person, she develops a sense of self-possession. She
knows where she stands in relation to other people,
especially the man in her life. The Tinker learns to
recognize the signs that indicate the foundation of a
productive and lasting relationship. Conversely, she
can identify cues indicating the onset of the Wendy
Dilemma. Even though you may exhibit some
Wendy responses, you can make a major break-
through in becoming a Tinker and resolving the
Wendy Dilemma by paying close attention to your
man's and your own behavior during the initial
stages of your encounter. In this way, you have an
excellent chance of desensitizing your fear of rejection and getting the relationship off on the right
track.

There are signs of a Peter Pan and Wendy relationship that appear soon after a man and woman
meet. I will review these, complete with examples
and advice on how you can convert the mothering
situation into an opportunity for adult growth. One
of my patients, a Tinker-in-training, was so excited
to be able to identify and profit from the problems
apparent in early courtship that she also helped her
man learn from the same situations. She didn't belittle or make fun of him, but it was with a good-
natured, tongue-in-cheek attitude that she said,
"You know, when a guy is first interested in a
woman, he's quite trainable."

The signs of immaturity and opportunity for

growth differ depending upon the phase of courtship. The following review and recommendations
assume that you are willing to critically evaluate not
only your man's behavior but your own as well.

NARCISSISM

Narcissism is often a part of an immature relationship. Some degree of narcissism may even occur
in a mature relationship. If it is recognized and
understood, it need not be an obstacle to adult
love.

Narcissism is a difficult concept to define. Drs.
Otto Kernberg and Helmut Kohut, who have
studied narcissism for many years, agree on certain
behavioral indices. The narcissist is diminished in
the ability to feel empathy and give love. Exploita-
tion of others for personal gain and grandiose ideas
characterizes the narcissist's pattern of living.
These are the characteristics of a severly disturbed
narcissist. Chances are that the kind of narcissism
you'll encounter will be more benign; it will focus
on exaggerated self-importance as a method of defense against feelings of insecurity.

Kernberg emphasizes that the narcissist has many
feelings of inferiority, and much narcissistic behavior is designed to hide those feelings. Although
most of the writings concerning narcissism seem to
imply that it is a male-dominated trait, the Wendy
woman is exhibiting a narcissistic tendency when
she hides behind the mothering image, pretending

to be competent, but in truth afraid to open herself to rejection.

If you are a Tinker-in-training, or wish to be, you'll want to be on the lookout for narcissism during all phases of the courtship. It can assume many forms. Here are a few.

Placation

Does he placate you? Do you placate him? When appeasement occurs in a normal conversation, one person is telling the other person, "I recognize that you are not as mature as I am, so I will humor you." The placator, in defense of feelings of inferiority, assigns him or herself a superior position and treats his or her companion like a naive little child.

See if the following excerpt from a conversation between a courting couple gives you a déjà vu experience.

She was in her early twenties and he was at least forty. They were snuggling in a corner booth in a restaurant, talking as if they were the only two people in the world.

WOMAN: "I would love to have a fur like that lady has."

MAN (surprised): "You would?"

WOMAN: "Sure, a lot of women dream of having a fur."

MAN (more surprised): "They do?"

WOMAN: "Oh, yes. It makes us feel so special."

MAN (leaning forward and squeezing her hand): "Wow."

The man was in his early forties, was dressed as if he'd just walked off the cover of *GQ*, was having dinner at a posh Los Angeles restaurant, and was pretending that he hadn't known some women dream of having a fur coat. Worse yet, the woman was going along with the charade. It seemed she was playing the same game when, about fifteen minutes later, the following exchange took place:

MAN (excited): "I'd love to have my own plane."

WOMAN: "Oh, I know."

MAN: "How would you know that I want one?"

WOMAN (motherly): "Because that's how guys are. You want your own plane just like I want my fur."

MAN: "God, you're really understanding."

My reaction to this scene is: "Why don't you two get out of the sandbox!"

These two "kids" were doing an excellent job of avoiding adult communication. They hid behind a shield of pretended maturity, placating one another. By feigning ignorance and then surprise, the man was setting himself up to be magnanimous. Later, he could say to himself, "Look how great I am. I showed the poor little woman that she could teach me something."

The woman placated the man. She set herself up as the naive little boy's mother, explaining to him how the world works. Later, she might think, "Look how wonderful I am. I was able to help a man toward a better understanding of the male-female relationship." Neither of them realized that they had set themselves up on a pedestal because they were afraid to be vulnerable.

If you find yourself or your man caught up in placation, you can break free of the superiority/inferiority complex by employing a combination of strategies. Silence, confrontation, humor, and changing the subject are effective methods for coping with placation.

When you hear evidence of placation, remain silent for a few seconds and then change the subject. The young woman in the restaurant could have used humor to confront her man's narcissism. When he expressed surprise at the suggestion that some women love fur, she might have replied in a gentle tone, "C'mon, don't play with me. I'm not in first grade and neither are you."

This type of confrontation could have led the couple into a productive conversation. They were trying to impress one another because they were feeling a little nervous. An honest disclosure of feelings would have stopped the narcissism and put their relationship back on solid ground. If they continued their mutual placation, it would only be a matter of time before their relationship would break up and they would be left with disappointment and regret.

Bragging

The Wendy woman tends to dismiss the bragging of her man as a necessary "male thing." Tinker, on the other hand, realizes that when a man brags, he places himself in a superior position to her. In that position he fails to listen and, more often than not, "takes" the conversation away from her. One woman explained to me how her date took the conversation away from her because he was so intent upon bragging about himself.

"We went out to dinner at this really nice restaurant. I had had a very exciting day at work and I was busting inside waiting to share it. It wasn't two minutes after I started talking about how I had managed a delicate personnel matter that he interrupted me and started talking about how he had manipulated some clients into buying some high-ticket items that they didn't even want.

"I sat there like a rock as he went on and on for maybe thirty minutes. Not only did he give me a complete history of how he had conned these smart-aleck guys, but he managed to tell me about all the new 'toys' he had recently purchased. We were halfway through our meal before I could get a word in edgewise. By then I was so disgusted with him, I didn't even want to share my story with him."

This woman tolerated her date's narcissism and bad manners. That was her mistake. If she had wanted to get the relationship off on the right track, she should have explained to him that she had some important things to share and wanted him to listen. As a Tinker, she might even have explained exactly what she expected. "I really want you to sit there and get into my day. I want you to appreciate my experiences as much as you can." If he had still interrupted her, she might have said, ''Please don't interrupt me right now. I need to talk.''

An even more directive confrontation was necessary for another woman, whose lover was a poor listener. Not only did he take the conversation away from her (once she tried to tell him about her new shoes and he told her that they weren't quite as rich in color as his shoes), but he also belittled her opinion whenever they tried to discuss such complicated matters as world affairs. He paid little attention to her gentle reminders and explanations. She finally became so exasperated that she confronted him directly. ''You say you care about me, but you treat me like dirt. You belittle and make fun of me and are so busy thinking about yourself that I might as well not exist. Show me more consideration or else I don't want any more to do with you.'' These were ''you messages'' but, in this case, necessary.

The following is one of my most instructive stories. It features a woman who was well on her way to becoming a Tinker. She had been dating a man for several weeks. They were lovers who seemed to genuinely enjoy each other's company. Note the veiled narcissism in her account of a critical incident.

''We had dinner on Wednesday evening and went back to my place to make love. We had a delightful evening. When he left he said he would call me that weekend.

''When he didn't call Friday or during the day Saturday, I made other plans for Saturday night and Sunday.

"He called me late Monday night and started making excuses about why he hadn't called on the weekend. I didn't say much. Then he said, 'Thanks for not getting mad at me for not calling you this weekend.'

"I really wasn't mad at him until he made that stupid comment. Then I was furious. I couldn't believe he was so self-centered. He really believed that I had nothing else to do with my life except sit around waiting for him to call me. And when he didn't, he figured I would be terribly upset.

"I told him that I resented his attitude toward me and that, while I cared for him, he certainly wasn't the center of my world. I think I shocked him."

The man's belief that his lover would be mad because he hadn't called expressed his narcissism. In effect he was saying, "I'm so important that, when I didn't call, you were obviously hurt at not being able to spend time with such a perfect person as myself."

Impulsiveness

Narcissism can lead you and your man into impulsive acts. He gets very excited about a good time you're having, so he says he loves you and wants to marry you. Yet that's the last you hear of him for two weeks. You get so excited about your sexual awakening that you agree to go on vacation with him to the Bahamas. The next morning, you regret your impulsiveness.

When you're convinced that your current thought

is the absolute truth, impulsive behavior is often the result. It's not fair to conclude that your man lied when he said he loved you or that you were being immoral when you said you wanted to spend a week alternating between sunbathing and making love. It's safe to say that you got carried away with the pleasures of the moment. That doesn't make you evil, just human.

The only rational way to recover from this relatively benign form of narcissism is to be honest. Your man need not beg for forgiveness—he simply needs to admit that, *at that moment*, he did want to marry you; unfortunately, the moment didn't last. And you don't have to justify the fact that you're still a modern woman despite your reluctance to have sex every moment of a dream vacation—you simply have to admit that, *at that moment*, you did want to make love for a week.

Honesty between lovers is an aphrodisiac. It is sensual, seductive, stimulating, and promotes ardor and endurance. Best of all, it is so special that honest lovers can make love for hundreds of hours, constantly discovering something new about each other.

MOTHERLINESS

I'll never forget the woman who taught me how any female can identify, with absolute certainty, that her man could easily become a Peter Pan, seducing her into becoming his Wendy. She explained it this way:

"We had been dating for several weeks and I found him charming and caring. He was fun to be with, though he tended to be a bit self-centered. I ignored his immaturity because he appeared to be so gentle.

"My entire perspective changed after he took me to his parents' house for dinner. They were wonderful people. His father was a sweet guy and his mother, though a bit formal, was very kind.

"You can imagine my shock when she took me into the kitchen and said, 'You're so good for my son. Ever since you've been dating him, he's been behaving himself like a gentleman. You're really helping him to shape up. I just hope you don't drop him. I don't know what I would do with him.''

This woman received a clear message that her man's mother still felt responsible for raising her son. One might say that she was passing the torch of motherhood to her son's girl friend. In her own way, the mother gave the woman a sign that the relationship was starting off on the *wrong* track.

An even clearer signal that your relationship is heading in the wrong direction can come from your own feelings, *provided* you are sensitive to them. The warning sign will be contained in a realization that you feel motherly toward your man. It is a multidimensional emotion rooted in a variety of circumstances.

- You seem to be constantly giving him attention without receiving any in return.

- You feel you must watch your words for fear of saying something that might offend him.
- You sense his weaknesses, but because he hides from them, you feel you must not criticize him.
- His cocky attitude and "macho man" character remind you of the boys you knew in high school.
- When you do criticize him, he has a way of making you feel guilty for opening your mouth in the first place.
- When he apologizes for a mistake, you feel sorry for him.

Any one of these circumstances can entice you into the Wendy trap. If you're honest with yourself, you should be able to identify a Wendy response and take remedial action. Confront each circumstance as it occurs, making sure that you communicate your thoughts and feelings as clearly as you can. In addition, tell your man what you would like to have him do to better the situation. Likewise, be willing to admit your shortcomings as well as talk about what you intend to do to correct them.

A woman sought my consultation several weeks after meeting a man she thought she loved and wanted to marry. The fact that many of her friends and co-workers were getting divorced scared her. She sought counseling so that she might avoid a similar fate. She summarized her goal this way: "I want you to give me 'second wife' lessons. I've heard that the second wife doesn't get the same little boy that the first wife had to endure. Give me second wife lessons so I'll know how to avoid the pitfalls of a first marriage. I don't want to be anybody's second wife.'' Becoming a Tinker gave her the protection she sought.

20
What to Expect When You Change

"I'm changing every day. I'm sure most of my friends think I'm nuts. But it's too late to turn back. They'll just have to adjust."

In her drive toward self-possession, Tinker makes a lot of mistakes. She overreacts to injustice, speaks her mind before having her thoughts in order, and occasionally forces herself to take action when relaxation is the best alternative. Despite her shortcomings, Tinker is heading in the right direction. She is becoming the best person she can be.

Although there are many positive benefits to becoming a Tinker, some of them are long-term. In the short-term, things sometimes get worse before they get better. Old friends become strangers, new friends become undependable, and new fears replace old ones. If you are in the process of resolving the Wendy Dilemma, you are well advised to consider some of the obstacles you must overcome on the road to becoming a Tinker.

A NEW SELF-IMAGE

Many women don't realize that they have lived with a negative self-image. In becoming a Tinker, they will gradually overcome the silent voice of inferiority and replace it with a voice of self-esteem. "I'm a good person and I deserve to be loved." With daily attention, the new self-image stimulates new ways of dealing with old problems. More effective patterns of conflict resolution feed the new self-image.

As your new self-image takes hold in your life, you can expect to experience a "roller coaster effect." That is, the highs that accompany a positive self-image will often lead to the lows that occur when the old, negative self-image rears its head. It's beneficial to realize that, because you are a creature of habit, your old, negative self-image is lurking in your memory, just waiting for the right moment to take control of your life.

When you get to the top of a roller coaster, you experience a thrill. Along with the excitement is the awareness of being in a precarious position. You know you must go down, but you're not sure when it will happen, how far you will drop, and how you'll react when you do drop. The new self-image will give you a dual sensation of excitement and apprehension. "What happens if I fall off?" is the threat stimulated by the remnants of the old self-image.

If you expect this sense of loss, you can anticipate it and not be dismayed when it occurs. As you understand the nature of yourself as a human being, you gain tolerance for temporary setbacks—the lows on the roller coaster. It is the nature of the new self-image to sometimes evaporate, often just when you need it the most. However, it's also the nature of a new self-image that the more you practice it, the stronger it becomes and the greater the likelihood that it will replace the old self-image, which grows weaker each time you accept it but refuse to follow it.

Here's one woman who struggled with the roller-coaster effect.

"This new man in my life is good for me. He respects me, communicates with me, and most of all, loves me for me. I want to marry him. I know it's right.

"But there's this other side of me. It says maybe I should go back to my ex-husband. Can you believe that? My ex was self-centered and immature. He lied to me and took me for granted and then had the nerve to say he loved me. And he hasn't changed. I don't believe that I would even think of going back to him. But I do. You can see why I think there's something seriously wrong with me."

There wasn't anything seriously wrong with this woman. On the contrary, she was becoming a Tinker. However, the Wendy within her was not letting go. That would take time. She was making two mistakes: She was expecting the new self-image to take complete control of her life within a few months; and she was damning herself for having moments of uncertainty about the new direction her life was taking. The solution to her roller-coaster experience was to first remind herself to have patience, and second, to practice accepting the Wendy within her (see Chapter 15).

CONFUSION

Probably the biggest hurdle to overcome in becoming a Tinker is learning to contend with the confusion that seems to rage inside your head. You got a glimpse of this confusion from the woman in the last section. She had thoughts of self-possession, independence, and self-control that were countered by ideas of returning to a lifestyle of subservience, disrespect, and mothering. Hope and contentment did battle with insecurity and fear of rejection.

A suggested reaction to this type of confusion is to *be glad you are confused.* Picture yourself walking down a path as you live out your life. You walk this path because you learned to and because you know what to expect. You will continue to walk it even though it causes you pain, simply out of the need for familiarity and the fear of change. But, if you see another path that crosses your old one, and through experimentation you discover that it promises some improvement in your life, are you not at a crossroads of sorts?

Your old path hasn't been all bad and you know the new path won't be filled with roses. Despite the discomfort, maybe the old path isn't so bad—at least you know what to expect. And maybe the new path won't deliver on its promises; or maybe you are expecting too much. Yet you long for change and the new path seems to lead in a more positive direction. Do you face the risk of the unknown by taking the new path or do you stay with the known dangers of the old path?

This confusion is good; it is healthy; and, to a woman wishing to become a Tinker, *it is necessary.* You can take heart in being confused, because it means you are seriously considering change. Change is *the* essential ingredient in growth and maturity. Without it, you cannot resolve the Wendy Dilemma. In this light, confusion is an emotional state that all growing people must learn to accept and work through.

You don't have to be happy with confusion. It certainly isn't a preferred emotion. But it does come with the territory of change. When you expect it, you'll seek to learn from it rather than fight it. The most convincing argument for accepting confusion is that, if you don't, it'll get worse. When you get confused about being confused, *then you're confused.*

POWER SURGE

When you take possession of your own life, you stop taking responsibility for the significant people in your life. You no longer seek to control the way other people react to you. You know that they are responsible for their own thoughts, feelings, and actions. When you were a Wendy, your control of life was misdirected. As you become a Tinker, along with the confusion of a new self-image, you'll likely experience a surge of power.

Freeing yourself from bondage opens you to a whole new way of looking at yourself. As we've seen in the last two sections, you can expect that this power surge will have its rough moments.

Listen to a woman telling me she had a tough time letting go.

"I hated you the day you told me there was nothing I could do to change my husband. I know it took months of you saying it before I heard it. But the day I finally heard it, I was devastated. I tried to blame you for being so cruel to me. But you weren't. It was just an overwhelming loss. Many people won't understand that. It was a sudden empty spot inside of me. It was worse than my miscarriage.

"After I recovered from the trauma, there was this strange feeling of exuberance inside of me. I wanted to go out and ride a motorcycle even though I'm scared to death of the damn things. I wanted to do something young and energetic—climb a mountain—I didn't care. The feeling of freedom was unbelievable. I didn't carry the guilt for his problems anymore. You told me I was carrying a heavy burden, but I never realized how heavy it was until I let go of it. God, the freedom!"

This woman's power surge also contained a roller-coaster effect. As she gave up trying to control her man's emotions, she felt a loss. If you are considering becoming a Tinker, it is wise to anticipate this loss.

As you accept the Wendy within you and help her overcome her fears, you will lose a part of you—a part that has been with you for a long time. Despite the fact that this part has held you back from growing, you will still feel bad at losing it. You may need to grieve the loss of Wendy as if she has died. For, in one respect, she has.

As you grieve, you will be hit with the realization that you have wasted precious time by hiding your fears behind Wendy. With that realization comes a difficult part of becoming a Tinker. Sadness. There's only one way to handle it—cry.

THE REACTION OF OTHERS

It's impossible to anticipate the range of people's reaction to your becoming a Tinker. Here are the key people and what you might expect from them.

Your Man

At the very least, the man in your life will have some adjustment to make to your new style of behavior. You should expect him to be confused, hurt, and maybe even bewildered. The degree of his confusion will depend upon the history of your relationship—how long you've been dating/married and how many Peter Pan and Wendy traits exist in your relationship. If your respective scores on the Peter Pan and Wendy quizzes were in the twenties, you should anticipate considerable adjustment difficulties.

The most likely outcome of your man's confusion is that he will try to make you return to your old style of behavior. He may do this because he's upset with you for changing the rules of the relationship, because his own insecurities demand the protection of your mothering, or because he simply doesn't want to face the inconvenience of learning new ways of relating to you.

You can expect to feel pressured into returning to your Wendy ways. "Why have you turned on me?" "Don't you love me anymore?" "You're backing away from your vows." These tactics create the pressure of guilt. Your old self-image may indeed agree with your man's evaluation, doubling the pressure you feel.

You can react to this pressure the same way you dealt with the roller-coaster effect; that is, by accepting the fact that change will spawn confusion and using the sharing procedures outlined in Chapter 17 to slowly adjust to change. You can explain that you haven't turned against him; you are, in fact, trying to love him even better; you probably are changing the rules of the relationship; and, indeed, they need changing.

This rational procedure may fail. Your man may employ radical measures in an attempt to blackmail you back into mothering. He may increase his drinking, blaming you. He may threaten to harm you or accuse you of having another man. He may vacillate between the extremes of crying and pleading and spouting vile accusations about everything you ever did wrong. He may threaten you with destitution only to turn around and buy you an exorbitant gift. (One man accused his wife of being a whore and then bought her a new sports car.) He may tell your friends that you are sick and destroying the marriage or try to turn the kids against you (see the next sections). Finally, he may run to his or your mother, hoping that either or both will pressure you into resuming your old Wendy ways.

Whatever the nature of the pressure you feel, the temptation to take responsibility for the entire problem will be tremendous. (A brief review of the "manure pile" analogy in Chapter 17 will help.) Recognizing the likelihood of one or more of these reactions coming from your man will prepare you. You can cope with it using your new self-image. If you find him to be totally irrational, you might have to leave the situation (temporarily or permanently). If he seems susceptible to logic, try talking. For example, when he says, "We wouldn't have these problems if it weren't for your 'liberation,' " you can say, "What you just said is an example of the kind of problems we need to solve. I don't cause your problems and I can't save you from them. However, I will admit that I am responsible for mothering you and misleading you into believing that I am the great savior of the world."

A bit of well-placed humor can help smooth the way for improved communication. Just remember not to make light of your problems or unintentionally belittle your man's confusion. Your humor will be beneficial if you remember to use gentle self-chiding, avoiding any reference to his behaving as your little boy. Those humorous comments should be saved for the time when he is willing to take an honest look at himself and take himself less seriously.

Throughout the strained interactions that are sure to result, be sure to remind your man and yourself that some of your troubles are caused by the fact that old habits die hard.

Your Children

If you have children, they too may put pressure on you to return to your old ways. And, as with your man, this pressure will most likely be manifested in guilt feelings. But take heart—they rarely do it on purpose.

When your educational program takes you away two evenings a week, your ten-year-old might say, "I want a full-time mother again. Do you have to go?" After assuring yourself that you're giving your kids plenty of love and guidance, you can respond, "I am your full-time mother, but I'm also a full-time person and I have other things I want to do." It also helps to remember that if you stayed home, chances are the ten-year-old would ignore you anyway.

When your job keeps you late and your five-year-old has tears in his eyes when he says, "I missed you, Mommy," banish the voices of guilt and reply, "I missed you too, honey." You needn't accuse yourself of neglect. Take this opportunity to talk with your husband about how he should be more involved with his children.

These same recommendations apply if you are becoming a Tinker and also are a single parent.

The most difficult problem you might encounter with your children is when your husband uses the kids to pressure you into your old ways. You'll want to hope that he does it unintentionally and will respond favorably to your request that he stop. If he's doing it intentionally and refuses to stop, then you'll be forced to add this to your list of reasons to leave (see the next chapter).

When your twelve-year-old says, "What are you doing to Dad?" you can say, "I'm only trying to love him better." When your eight-year-old asks, "Don't you love Daddy anymore?" you can reply, "Absolutely. That's why I'm trying to become a better person."

Keep in mind that it's not your responsibility to explain your husband's behavior to your children; it's his.

Your Friends and Acquaintances

Friends, acquaintances, and co-workers will have a variety of reactions to the new you. Your new self-image will be put to the test on a daily basis.

Your neighbor friend may chastise you for "being so cruel to that great husband you've got." Your best friend might have a note of disapproval in her voice when she says, "Are you *sure* you know what you're doing?" Jealousy might be the motivating force when a co-worker says, "I know I wouldn't risk losing a good thing if I had it." Your boss might shake your confidence by misreading your new self-image as an indication of problems: "Is there anything bothering you?" A casual friend might search for gossip by pressing you for details: "And then what did you say? And what did he say?"

Faced with these confrontations, you'll be tempted to psychologize as to the motivation behind the comments and questions. You can put your curiosity to rest by realizing that a true friend will support you in any way he or she can, and the others have a mixture of motives, not the least of which are jealousy because you're doing what they want to do, and fear because your courage might shake them out of their lethargy, or make them confront their own denial.

If you wish to reduce the wear and tear on your new self-image, make a simple decision ahead of time. That is, if you feel a person's concern is sincere and deserving of an explanation, give it to him or her. If not, simply rehearse a one-line response that is pleasant and humorous, but doesn't tell them anything you don't want them to know. For example, "I guess I'm just getting an early jump on the change of life."

Your Parents

If your parents are still living, you'll face a difficult time when they ask you what is happening. Once again, their questions and comments can provoke guilt. If you have yet to resolve your dependency upon your mother or the feelings of rejection that you felt from your father, their questions or comments can cause you to respond with anger.

When dealing with your parents, give yourself and them ample compassion, understanding, and forgiveness. When combining the stress of becoming a Tinker with the frustration of unresolved dependency needs toward your parents, you can expect yourself to say something you wish you hadn't.

To eliminate some of the hassle, follow the same course of action you did with your friends and co-workers. That is, make up your mind ahead of time how much information you want to give to each parent. Realize that if you tell them half the story, they'll probably push you for the other half. In that case, you should decide before the fact whether or not you want to talk about how you believe their mistakes contributed to your problems. If you share those innermost feelings, be prepared to hear their guilt, denial, or other emotional reactions to your disclosures. Likewise, take great care in explaining how you aren't blaming them for your problems. Emphasize that you don't want to live in the past.

Many ex-Wendy women decide against sharing any depth with their parents. They conclude that their mother and father have lived their lives to the best of their abilities and there is nothing to be gained by opening up a whole new vista that would only serve to confuse rather than clarify. You can become a Tinker without analyzing why you became a Wendy. In fact, a full-fledged Tinker has little time for historical analysis.

BIASED SHRINKS

As you become a Tinker, you'll feel the need for objective guidance. Finding an unbiased psychiatrist, psychologist, social worker, or other counselor (shrink) can be one of the best investments you can possibly make in your future. However, you must be very careful when seeking a shrink. You, better than anyone, know that you are in a delicate position, made vulnerable by your uncertainty. The last thing you need is a biased shrink using you to act out his or her own hang-ups.

One woman who went to a male psychotherapist was made to feel guilty for wanting to become more independent. The shrink said, "Don't confront your husband. When he comes in at three A.M., make him a sandwich and coffee and tell him how much you missed him." The only way to deal with this kind of advice is *not* to go back.

In seeking a shrink, be aware of the following.

Chauvinism

The advice given by the therapist above is a good example of male chauvinism. Just as dangerous is the advice given by a female chauvinist. She may suggest that you take a certain course of action, not because she has considered your clinical history objectively, but because she wishes to act out her own frustrations using you as a guinea pig.

Shoulds

If the counselor you choose is constantly referring to what you *should* do, implying that there is only one way to become a Tinker (his or her way), consider finding another professional helper. When you are in the process of throwing away the mothering script, the last thing you need is a person you trust giving you another script.

Sex

To repeat something that bears repeating: *There is no way you can get objective therapy and sex from a therapist.*

Money

You don't necessarily have to spend eighty or ninety dollars an hour to find good counseling. Local governmental agencies, church groups, universities, and private clinics often have reputable therapists available on an ability-to-pay basis.

Shop Around

Talk to your trusted friend, your physician, or your minister in searching for a shrink. Many communities have referral services that help you find the kind of therapist you're looking for. You can also use the Yellow Pages. Get two or three names and call. Ask the receptionist or the counselor a few questions. For example: What theories do you use in counseling people? Can I have longer than an hour if I want it? What experience have you had with women going through an identity crisis? Any counselor, or his or her representative, who will not take a few minutes to talk with you about these things probably isn't worth seeing.

Don't be afraid to shop around. Just because you need help doesn't mean you're helpless.

SEXUALITY REBORN

A dedication to taking charge of one's life combined with a new positive self-image can lead to a rebirth of sexuality. As you resolve your Wendy Dilemma, climb out of the Wendy trap, reduce your Wendy responses, and increase your Tinker behavior, you may find a whole new world of sexual need emerging within you.

The main reason for this increased sex drive is your new self-image. You like yourself more and realize you deserve to enjoy yourself. You can expect to look forward to sex, to want satisfaction for yourself as well as your mate, to forego the old practice of just lying there and faking orgasms, to occasionally feel frustrated when sexual fulfillment is lacking, to become aggressive before and during sexual activity, to have daydreams filled with sexual scenes, and, atypically, to find yourself smiling to yourself because a man turned *you* down.

The rebirth of your sexuality isn't cause for alarm or guilt. You may feel a bit self-conscious as you reexamine old values, but chances are you needn't worry about becoming promiscuous. As you've done with other growth experiences, give yourself patience and understanding.

Anticipating these obstacles and rehearsing possible strategies doesn't make becoming a Tinker an easy task. There will always be experiences that rekindle the Wendy Dilemma. But expecting certain things to occur can make the task easier. Yet despite the best of all possible preparation, the unexpected will occur—probably when you least expect it.

21

When and How to Leave

"There comes a time, no matter how much guilt you feel, when you just have to get out. The toughest part is wondering if you're doing the right thing."

Despite its title, this chapter, like the ones before, contains a message of hope. It is presented to those women who have resolved the Wendy Dilemma—to love, not mother—but without success. Their man refuses to grow up and they can no longer keep their life on "hold." They want to give their love to a person who will be nourished by it and who will give love in return.

Leaving, even to the self-possessed Tinker, can be an emotional nightmare. Unless her man is some kind of sadist, she will experience regret, fear, guilt, and more. If she has a history of mothering him, her uncertainty and confusion will create a voice inside of her that says, "Are you *sure* you know what you're doing? Maybe just one more try."

Even if she doesn't love him, leaving is not as simple as saying, "I'm looking for an apartment." After all, he *was* family and your home *was* your nest. When a Wendy-becoming-a-Tinker leaves a

relationship, she walks away from a certain degree
of security and submits herself to new dimensions
of life. Unless she is walking into another man's
arms (not necessarily a good idea—she could easily
repeat her past mistakes), she will encounter a
highly stressful period of her life. She'll want to
know, to the best of her ability, that she's doing the
right thing.

When women ask me to help them decide whether or not to leave their relationship, I lead them
through an objective checklist. It doesn't promise
perfection, but it gives them confidence that, if they
leave and things don't go well, they can reassure
themselves by saying, "I know I gave my last relationship my best shot."

Here is the checklist.

• *Do you care enough about him to work on your
  problems?*

  Many women say they still love their man,
  even though the X factor is no longer func-
  tional. They feel sorry for him or feel afraid of
  leaving, but they don't love him. However, if
  these women are sitting in my office, they
  probably have enough love left to go on to the
  second step in the checklist.

• *Do you know what your mistakes are?*

  Women who are thinking of leaving usually
  go to one extreme or the other in reaction to this
  question. Either they have little sensitivity to
  their mistakes, or they are so riddled with guilt

that they rattle off their errors like a well-rehearsed child going to his first confession.

Neither extreme is a solid basis for leaving. This part of the checklist requires a woman to analyze a troublesome situation and identify her self-defeating thoughts and actions. If she says she mothered him, then she must identify which of the Wendy responses apply to her. If she can't be specific in self-criticism, then she won't be able to fulfill the expectations of the next step in the checklist.

• *Did you try your best to correct your mistakes?*

At this point in the checklist, I review several situations to see if the woman did, in fact, employ rational problem-solving techniques. Much as a tutor would do in reviewing homework, I help her evaluate the range of techniques used with an eye to assuring her that she implemented the technique correctly. Most of the techniques I teach are contained in the second section of the book or in the readings outlined in the Appendix.

• *Did you seek objective feedback regarding your situation?*

In the case of the woman sitting in my office, her very presence answers this question. For the reader, ''objective feedback'' will not come from your friends or family. Use the suggestions contained in Chapter 20 in the section on unbiased shrinks to find someone who can help you evaluate the issues raised in this chapter.

- *Did you try to get him to go for help?*

    Many men still believe that "you can solve your own problems; you don't need a shrink." Other men use this as an excuse to avoid the anxiety of self-examination. Before leaving, you owe it to your relationship to do your best to encourage your man to seek counseling, with or without you.

If you can sincerely answer yes to all five of these questions, and your relationship is not improving, then you may very well consider implementing the steps outlined in the rest of this chapter, steps suggesting when and how to leave. Be advised that these steps are recommended for a woman whose relationship has some semblance of human decency left to it. They are not germane to a woman who faces abuse or threat of abuse. If the latter is the case, the woman may want to consult the special advice contained in step two.

STEP ONE: A LAST STAND

A couple I was seeing for marriage counseling were a typical Peter Pan and Wendy. Together we had been focusing on changing specific situations around the house. They both said the right words, but neither seemed dedicated to correcting their respective mistakes.

Several weeks into marriage counseling, the woman announced that she was leaving. Despite their long-standing problems, the woman had never seriously mentioned the subject. The husband was flabbergasted. He was still in shock when he walked out of my office.

The next week, he came in by himself. His wife had already moved out and filed for divorce. He was still in shock. "I never thought she'd do it. I'm willing to admit my mistakes and get serious about counseling. But she says she doesn't care anymore." He looked miserable. "After seventeen years of marriage, she finally takes a stand, and it's her last stand."

If you take a last stand, do it *before* you don't care anymore. Do it while you still feel hope for the relationship. This was expressed by one woman who said, "I'm in love with what I know he could be, not what he is now." She took her last stand while she still cared whether or not it worked.

When taking your last stand, make sure you state your concerns and intentions about leaving as unequivocally as possible. In other words, don't beat around the bush. Likewise, maintain the most rational posture you can, free from wild emotions. Write him a letter and read it to him if you must. You'll want to maximize the chances that he will hear you.

Consult an attorney regarding your rights. He or she may advise you about ways to get your husband to leave. If there are children involved and they will stay with you, it is best for their adjustment if they remain in the family home.

Take a very hard look at your financial options. You have probably been involved in the ongoing process of personal development suggested in previous chapters. You'll need a budget to bolster your confidence when walking out the door (or if he walks out).

Say little to the children about your plans, but be willing to answer their questions. If they ask you, "Are you getting a divorce?" tell them you're working hard to avoid such a thing.

The crux of your last stand is the statement. "If we don't start working on our problems, I'm leaving." Don't say this until and unless you mean it.

STEP TWO: LEAVING

Many women stay in a relationship because they are petrified of the physical and logistical aspects of leaving. Here are the reflections of a woman who had stayed too long.

"I just want him to leave me alone. He can sit in front of the television twenty-four hours a day for all I care. Just as long as he doesn't try to talk to me.

"The only thing I need him for is his paycheck, which isn't great by the way, and occasionally as a babysitter. If only I could not get mad at him, then I'd stay right where I am."

This woman's denial was closing in around her. The Wendy trap was suffocating her. Despite her fears about not being able to support herself and her two kids, this woman did leave; at last report, she was making it.

You can reduce some of the fear of leaving by finding ways to invest in your future. If you stay in your present home, rearrange the furniture and, as your budget allows, redecorate parts of the house. For example, move a chair from the family room to your bedroom, learn how to hang wallpaper and give your bedroom a different atmosphere, or buy some new piece of furnishing, even if it comes from a secondhand store.

You may move into a new place. Listen to how one woman built herself a new nest:

"Walking into a new apartment is kind of like going to a wake. It can make you long for your old house, no matter how bad the ghosts might be. All I could think of was how unfair he'd been not to change. I blamed him for making me leave.

"I was so destroyed by self-pity, I sat in this empty room and cried. Then I got mad at myself and reminded myself why I left.

"I went out and bought a new picture and unpacked some of my personal decorations. I got myself a bottle of wine and had a private housewarming party. I hung up my kitchen utensils and ordered a pizza. I sat on the floor playing music that he never liked. It still wasn't great, but it was a new start."

If you face physical threats, you won't have the luxury of suffering your way through the emotional roller coaster associated with building a new nest. You'll be too worried about your safety. If you speak of leaving and your man threatens to harm you, take the threat seriously. Any person who would stoop to threats of physical violence is unbalanced enough to follow through.

If you legitimately fear for your safety, evaluate your alternatives *before* making any final statements to your husband. Talk to a counselor, an attorney, a judge, the police, or social agencies about ways of insuring your protection if leaving becomes a reality. Don't cower in the corner, afraid to take a stand; on the other hand, don't try to prove that you can stand alone.

STEP THREE: OVERCOMING THE HURDLES

When you decide to leave, there are countless hurdles to overcome. Here are just a few.

Kids

If you have children, odds are that they will stay with you. How do you tell them about leaving? What do you say about their father? What do you say about your reasons for leaving? How much information should you give them? A general rule to follow is to answer the children's questions in simple terms, giving them only the information they request. If you are in doubt as to what they want to know, ask leading questions that will clarify their need for information.

Do not damn their father or go into excessive detail about your marital difficulties. Maintain a sensible level of rational discipline, granting exception to the rules only after the children have demonstrated proper behavior. Expect them to carry a little more of a share of responsibility and never give them pity.

If their father says negative things about you to the kids or fails to give the children the time and attention they deserve, simply explain to the kids that their father is having some problems and his behavior is *not* their fault.

Friends and Family

When you go through the stress of leaving, you'll find out in a hurry who your true loved ones are. You'll need the support of some friends and/or family. There should be at least one person in your immediate surroundings who'll give you an ear for listening and a shoulder to cry on.

As for those who ask probing questions, follow the advice given in the last chapter. Decide ahead of time with whom you will share what information and under what circumstances. You may have a tendency to give too many people too much information, so take your time in deciding whom you will trust.

Seeing Him

Despite the nasty things he might have said to you, there is an excellent chance that your husband will call, write, or show up on your doorstep, filled with apologies and promises of change. In addition to the suggestions given in step four—reconciliation—

here are a few other ideas that might ease the burden of those encounters.

- If you want to talk with your husband, do it on neutral ground (a coffee shop). That way you minimize the likelihood of an argument and make it easy for yourself to leave if the meeting turns sour.
- Listen carefully to your man's words. Is he honestly admitting his mistakes or seeking help to change? Is the same old little-boy quality still there? Here is a prime example of a promise that indicates no change: "I'll even start feeling if you want me to."
- As suggested in Chapter 17, do your best to stick with "I messages"; for example, "I feel uncomfortable with your pushing me to make up my mind about returning."
- Do not drink alcohol during these first meetings.
- Be prepared to think fondly of him; the mind has a tendency to quickly forget pain. Fond thoughts are necessary but not enough to rebuild a relationship.
- Keep the children away from these meetings.
- Do *not* ask him if he's dating. You will feel jealous, and there's no reason to endure unnecessary emotional pain.

Money

Even if you have an excellent job, you'll probably need some type of financial aid and/or information. The lack of money is a very real problem, but with determination and expert guidance it need not be an insurmountable hurdle. Your friends, your banker, your co-workers, and your boss can provide you with support and ideas for getting help. As a Tinker, don't be embarrassed to ask. Gene Mackevich's *The Woman's Money Book* can be of some help (see Appendix).

Stress

Leaving a relationship ranks at or near the top of every list of stressful events. Even if things go smoothly, leaving is a situation filled with stress. You are well advised to accept the fact that your sleep may be fitful, your tolerance for inconvenience may be low, your patience may be thin, and your resistance to colds and flu decreased.

To cope with this stress, give yourself at least thirty minutes a day just to sit and relax; seek a physician's advice about an exercise program and a vitamin-supplemented diet; resist the temptation to constantly entertain the children, or if you're childless don't feel you must act out all your fantasies within a week; and be very careful not to become dependent upon alcohol or other drugs. Continuing with your counseling for several weeks is an excellent way to monitor your handling of stress.

STEP FOUR: RECONCILIATION

If you left while you still had some hope for the relationship, then reconciliation is always in the back of your mind. Since one of the purposes of leaving was to reevaluate your relationship, there are some guidelines you should follow during your separation.

- Resist the temptation to get involved with a new man. If it happens, then fate has spoken; but don't go looking for it. One rule many women follow is, if they see other men, they don't date them three times in a row.
- Spend time alone. The sounds of silence can teach you many things about the direction your life should take.
- If you meet with your man, avoid ''serious talks'' for a few weeks. If you date him, try to have fun.
- If and when you have sex, expect to experience a broad spectrum of emotions, from guilt to exhilaration. If the sex is with your man, expect to experience considerable confusion.
- You should have a goal *for yourself* to achieve during the separation. If your only objective is to give him time to think, then you run the risk of wasting time.

If you decide to reconcile with your man, it must be done with the understanding that you will both dedicate yourselves to intensive marriage counseling. Despite your hopes for a new beginning, you will have many bad habits to overcome. That will require teamwork, the likes of which you've probably never had with your man.

Appendix:
Helpful Reading

The following books are relevant to the resolution of feelings of rejection and inferiority, to the achievement of a positive self-image, and to the maintenance of an egalitarian relationship between a woman and her man. Though the list is not exhaustive, these books will add depth to your understanding of the dynamics of the Wendy Dilemma and, in many cases, provide you with creative ideas for becoming a Tinker.

Appleton, Jane, and William Appleton. *How Not to Split Up*. New York: Berkley, 1979.

Among the topics covered are overcoming boredom, recognizing and resolving self-centeredness, constructive use of leisure time, and pathways to mature sexuality. This book is filled with commonsense ideas, is easy to read, and could prove quite beneficial provided both of you read the book and implement the recommendations.

Benson, Herbert, with Miriam Klipper. *The Relaxation Response*. New York: Avon, 1976.

This book teaches you the many ways to relax. You'll learn to identify the internal signs of stress, to control your thoughts, and to grasp the fundamentals of meditation. These skills are essential for the self-possessed person.

Berne, Eric. *Games People Play.* New York: Grove, 1964.

This is a basic primer in transactional analysis, a method of viewing social interaction as a series of "games." The case histories are informative and new concepts are clearly defined. The book contains help in identifying destructive patterns of behavior. However, the author could have included more in the way of concrete suggestions for change.

Bessell, Harold. *The Love Test.* New York: Morrow, 1984.

A very helpful book for anyone seeking to define in behavioral terms the adult love script (although many readers may shy away from a precise evaluation of their "love" for another human being). In addition to containing a lot of information, the book is also fun to read.

Bloomfield, Harold, with Leonard Felder. *Making Peace with Your Parents.* New York: Random House, 1983.

This book includes case histories of people who have made peace with their parents. Most beneficial are suggestions for breaking free of the dire need for parental approval, dealing with anger toward one's parents, and coping with the challenges of aging parents. Anyone seeking to resolve dependency needs will benefit from this book's lessons in viewing your parents in a new light. Dr. Bloomfield's recommendation that *you* need to modify your reaction to your parents because *they* probably won't change seems a bit simplistic. However, this is an upbeat book with many good insights.

Brownmiller, Susan. *Femininity*. New York: Linden Press/Simon and Schuster, 1984.

This is a critical review of the role structures that define femininity and are too often blindly accepted by women. If a woman wishes to reexamine her femininity, this book will seriously challenge most of her current beliefs and practices. My only argument with this heavily historical work is that everything a woman does seems to be wrong. When reading this book, optimism will have to be supplied by the reader.

Burns, David. *Feeling Good: The New Mood Therapy*. New York: Signet, 1981.

Perhaps the best book on the innovations in cognitive therapy, an approach that can be very helpful in resolving the Wendy Dilemma. Dr. Burns take the "power of positive thinking" beyond the inspirational and into the scientific.

Dowling, Colette. *The Cinderella Complex*. New York: Pocket Books, 1982.

This book about women's fear of independence is essential reading for anyone seeking to become a Tinker. After all, remaining a Wendy is one way women avoid independence.

Ellis, Albert. *The Art and Science of Love*. New York: Lyle Stuart, 1960.

This is a practical guide to lovemaking. Written in Dr. Ellis's honest and forthright manner, this book's relevancy remains intact after over twenty years. Chapter 7, "Sexual Intercourse: Psychological Foundations," should be must reading for all lovers.

Fromm, Erich. *The Art of Loving*. New York: Bantam, 1963.

Just as Dr. Bessell defines the behaviors of love, Dr.

Fromm defines the philosophy of loving. This classic contains such statements as: "The deepest need of man, then, is the need to overcome his separateness, to leave the prison of his aloneness." "Without love, humanity could not exist for a day."

Harris, Thomas. *I'm OK—You're OK*. New York: Harper and Row, 1967.
This is a popular treatment of transactional analysis. Anyone wishing to understand the internal dynamics of Wendy, Tinker, and unresolved voices from the past will find doable advice in this book.

Kiley, Dan. *The Peter Pan Syndrome*. New York: Dodd, Mead, 1983.
A critical look at a widespread phenomenon in which men reach adult age but lack mature behaviors. The author places emphasis upon how a Peter Pan behaves, how his developmental history accounts for his actions, what can be done to overcome the syndrome, and how the woman in his life can help.

Kopp, Sheldon B. *If You Meet the Buddha on the Road, Kill Him!* New York: Bantam, 1976.
A very serious and eye-opening look at the pilgrimage of being a therapy patient. It is must reading for anyone investing time and money in psychotherapy. Although alarming, the title reflects the theme of the book: eliminate (by not returning to) any therapist who acts as if he or she has all the answers to your problems.

Mackevich, Gene. *The Woman's Money Book*. New York: Bantam, 1981.
This book will help a woman start thinking about her financial future. Although the constantly changing tax laws may have made some of his suggestions obsolete,

the reader can still gain an understanding for the necessity of taking control of financial matters. The book is heavily laden with investment information, but doesn't help much with budget matters.

May, Rollo. *The Discovery of Being*. New York: Norton, 1983.

If you are at all philosophical in your thinking, this book will help you put yourself in the middle of a practical evaluation of anxiety and the deeper, long-lasting solutions to isolation and loneliness.

Meichenbaum, Donald. *Cognitive Behavior Modification: An Integrative Approach*. New York: Plenum Press, 1977.

This is a textbook that will be understandable to the informed layperson. It adds considerable substance to the popular books written by Burns and Peale.

Missildine, Hugh. *Your Inner Child of the Past*. New York: Pocket, 1982.

This book will help you understand and accept the Wendy that lives within you. The author notes that it's okay if a part of us remains a child—it's even normal and desirable. The author draws continual parallels between present-day self-defeating behavior and problems experienced as a child.

Orbach, Susie. *Fat Is a Feminist Issue*. New York: Berkley, 1979.

The book jacket says it all: "Fat is not about food. Fat is about protection, sex, mothering, strength, assertion and love. You can change your response by learning the difference between 'mouth hunger' and 'stomach hunger.' "

Peale, Norman Vincent. *The Power of Positive Thinking*. New York: Fawcett Crest, 1963.
Dr. Peale uses quotes from Scripture and general theological references to support his inspirational message. You need not be a Christian or even a theist to profit from this classic work.

Phillips, Gerald, and Lloyd Goodall. *Loving and Living*. Englewood Cliffs, N.J.: Prentice-Hall, 1983.
Two professors of communications interviewed over four thousand men and women. A few of their conclusions are: Men don't think of their wives as their best friends; women want men to protect them as well as give them support and romance; many love relationships are filled with hostility and mistrust; and most men expect dedication, servile attention, sensuality, and sexual skill from their woman.

Russianoff, Penelope. *Why Do I Think I Am Nothing without a Man?* New York: Bantam, 1982.
Many women have said that this book has touched them with its realistic insight. It is a good first step to understanding one dynamic of the Wendy Dilemma. The author inspires you to become a whole person and to own your life. Much of what the author speaks of might be called "self-possession."